THE DISTANT DRUM
Reflections on the Spanish Civil War

'How sweet is mortal Sovranty!' – think some:
Others – 'How blest the Paradise to come!'
Ah, take the Cash in hand and waive the Rest;
Oh, the Brave Music of a distant Drum!

Rubaiyat of Omar Khayyam

THE DISTANT DRUM

Reflections on the Spanish Civil War

edited by

PHILIP TOYNBEE

SIDGWICK & JACKSON
LONDON

First published in Great Britain by Sidgwick and Jackson Limited

ISBN 0 283 98315 9

Printed in Great Britain by
The Garden City Press Limited
Letchworth, Hertfordshire SG6 1JS
for Sidgwick and Jackson Limited
1 Tavistock Chambers, Bloomsbury Way
London WC1A 2SG

Contents

Illustrations

All photographs except for * and † are reproduced by kind permission of Popperfoto. We are grateful to Alfred Lent for the use of the remaining two.

Introduction

PHILIP TOYNBEE

When a group of Spanish generals rose against the Republican government of Spain in July 1936, the enterprise might well have seemed foolhardy in the extreme to anyone who knew nothing about the international situation of that time. The four major powers of Western Europe were divided into two ideologically hostile camps. Britain and France were liberal parliamentary democracies; Italy and Germany were ruled by fascist and National Socialist regimes, which made them natural authoritarian allies of the Right.

But ever since Hitler had come to power in 1933 these two camps had been very unevenly matched, though in two diametrically opposite respects. So far as actual military power went, the democracies were far stronger than a Germany which had only partially rearmed herself, even that being contrary to the prohibitions imposed on her in 1919, and an Italy which was known to be inhabited by a profoundly unmilitary people, in spite of Mussolini's attempt to turn them into warriors, and in spite of his successful Abyssinian campaign of 1935–6.

Yet on the vaguer but no less important issue of political morale these positions were exactly reversed. Britain was governed by a supposedly National government, but this alliance of the moderate Right showed no self-confidence except in its harsh treatment of the two million British unemployed. France had been shaken by the Stavisky scandal of 1934, a revelation of extensive corruption in high places, and was sharply divided between the socialist-communist government and its supporters on the one hand, and the small but ferocious organizations of the extreme Right on the other. But Germany and Italy, however much their regimes may have been fated to self-destruction in the long run, were still bursting with aggressive self-assurance and faith in their own strength.

As for the two super-powers of our own time, America had deliberately excluded herself from European affairs by her refusal to join the League of Nations when it was formed immediately after the First World War, and Russia under Stalin had turned inward on herself and was taking relatively little interest in the successes or failures of foreign communist parties. Stalin's henchmen were largely preoccupied with killing each other off under the wayward direction of their master.

What all this means is that the two most dynamic governments in Europe were likely to be strongly sympathetic to Franco's cause in Spain, while the Republicans, though hoping against hope for massive Russian assistance and for at least the friendly neutrality of Britain and France, would have to rely on very weak reeds indeed.

Soon after the outbreak of the war a 'Non-intervention' policy was signed at Geneva, by which Germany, Italy, France and Britain agreed to let the Spaniards fight it out with no interference from the outside. This policy was a farce from the beginning. Italy sent whole divisions of 'volunteers' to fight for Franco, Germany sent technicians, pilots, and a large supply of war material. By strong contrast Britain and France strictly observed the terms of the agreement, and even discouraged genuine volunteers from making their own way to Spain. As for Russia, although she certainly sent tanks, aircraft and technicians her support of the Republic was always lukewarm: Stalin was far more interested in helping the Spanish Communist Party against its supposed allies and in making sure that the leaders of that party were irreproachable servants of the Soviet Union.

But in addition to their virtual certainty that they would soon receive massive aid from Germany and Italy the Spanish generals also had the advantage of controlling nearly all the Spanish armed forces. And in the event the general history of the two-and-a-half-year war was one of inexorable advance by Franco's forces, punctuated by a few relatively ineffective counter-attacks by the relatively untrained forces of the Republic. The only really notable military feat of the Spanish

Republic was to keep a precarious hold on Madrid right up to the bitter end.

The revolt began with concerted *coups* on the peripheries of Spain – in the Canary Islands, in Andalusia and, most powerfully, in Spanish Morocco. By the end of 1936, already greatly helped by outside intervention, Franco's forces had occupied nearly the whole of northern and western Spain. A year later they had conquered the Basque country in the north, and south-western Spain up to a line running from Granada to Cordoba. A year later again they had reached the Mediterranean coast and cut off Barcelona and its immediate hinterland from the rest of Republican Spain. This enclave was overrun between December 1938 and February 1939, by which time the Republic, which was finally beaten into unconditional surrender a month later, controlled only the south-eastern third of the country.

The most notable Republican counter-attacks had been made by the Catalan anarchists in August 1936; by the newly formed International Brigade on the Jarama ridge to the south-east of Madrid in February 1937; by Spaniards and Brigaders against the Italians at Guadalajara a month later; and by mixed Republican forces at Teruel in September 1937. Of course there were successful skirmishes here and there, and heroic individual actions everywhere (and on both sides), and there was the brave and skilful defence of Madrid right up to the moment of total Republican collapse, but all the great and lasting advances were made by Franco's troops and their allies – aided in this not only by direct foreign support but also by a successful Nationalist naval blockade of Republican Spain.

* * *

This book is partly about these major events and issues of the Spanish Civil War, but most of the material assembled here has been written by eyewitnesses who were more concerned with the trees than with the wood. Neither the historians nor the participants have told the whole story, partly because whole stories are never told and because nearly all the contributors to this book are British. Yet a reader will very soon discover that this shared nationality has imposed no homogeneity of attitude or emotion. Of the three major contributors, apart from myself, Mr Crozier and Mr Cockburn would agree on little more than the fact that a war did actually take place, in Spain and at that time. Professor Thomas, whose excellent history of the war is still the best general account, holds the balance here.

The object of this book is to present the war as vividly and as fairly as possible. It is true that a majority of the contributors are better disposed to the Republican than to the Nationalist cause: so were the majority of Englishmen at the time when the war was being fought. Nothing is settled here; there are no great and new revelations; it is not the intention of this symposium to win readers' support for either side. Auden ended his fine contemporary poem on Spain with the following verse:

> The stars are dead. The animals will not look.
> We are left alone with our day, and the time is
>   short and History to the defeated
> May say Alas but cannot help nor pardon.*

Whether we mourn with the defeated or rejoice with the victors on this fortieth anniversary of the generals' revolt it would surely be wrong to imitate Auden's animals. Whatever the rights and wrongs of the Spanish Civil War, whatever its historical meaning, this is a tragedy of the recent past which deserves our attention. Perhaps history never helps or pardons the defeated, but it should not overlook them any more than it overlooks their conquerors.

* Spain *W. H. Auden*

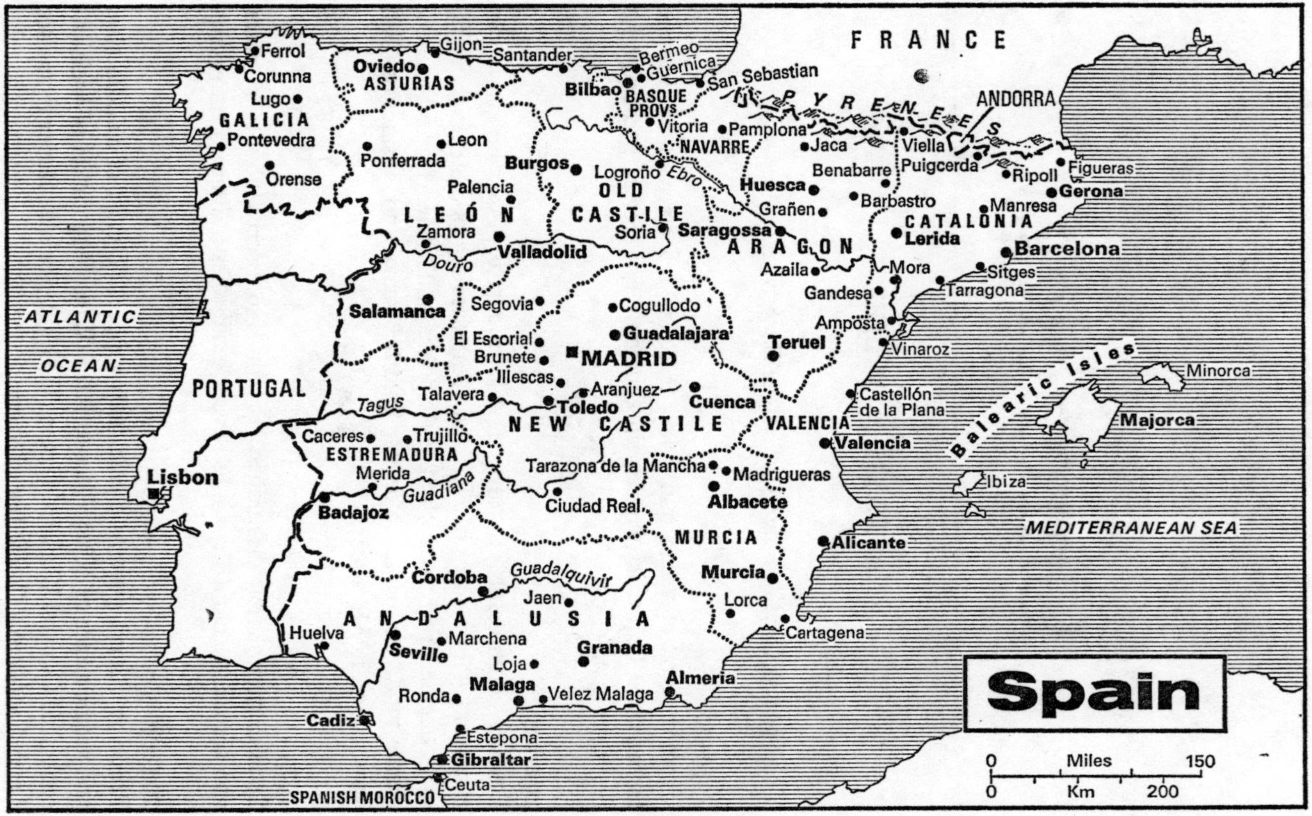
Spain
FRANCE
ANDORRA
PYRENEES
ATLANTIC OCEAN
MEDITERRANEAN SEA
PORTUGAL
SPANISH MOROCCO
Balearic Isles
Minorca
Majorca
Ibiza
GALICIA
ASTURIAS
BASQUE PROVS.
NAVARRE
LEÓN
OLD CASTILE
ARAGON
CATALONIA
NEW CASTILE
VALENCIA
ESTREMADURA
MURCIA
ANDALUSIA
Ferrol
Corunna
Lugo
Pontevedra
Orense
Oviedo
Gijon
Santander
Bilbao
Bermeo
Guernica
San Sebastian
Vitoria
Pamplona
Jaca
Viella
Puigcerda
Ripoll
Figueras
Gerona
Leon
Ponferrada
Burgos
Logroño
Ebro
Palencia
Zamora
Valladolid
Douro
Soria
Saragossa
Huesca
Benabarre
Barbastro
Grañen
Manresa
Lerida
Barcelona
Sitges
Tarragona
Mora
Azaila
Gandesa
Amposta
Vinaroz
Salamanca
Segovia
Cogullodo
El Escorial
Guadalajara
Brunete
MADRID
Illescas
Teruel
Talavera
Tagus
Toledo
Aranjuez
Cuenca
Castellón de la Plana
Lisbon
Caceres
Trujillo
Valencia
Merida
Guadiana
Tarazona de la Mancha
Madrigueras
Albacete
Badajoz
Ciudad Real
Alicante
Cordoba
Guadalquivir
Jaen
Murcia
Lorca
Cartagena
Huelva
Seville
Marchena
Granada
Loja
Malaga
Velez Malaga
Almeria
Ronda
Cadiz
Estepona
Gibraltar
Ceuta
0 Miles 150
0 Km 200

Chronology

BASIL COLLIER

The Spanish Civil War and its Political Background

1916–20
Upward spiral of wages and prices in Spain reflects wartime demand for exports. Industrial workers in Catalonia outnumber peasantry for first time in any Spanish province.

1921–2
Postwar slump hits Catalan textile industry. Anarcho-syndicalist extremists gain control of National Confederation of Labour (C.N.T.) in Catalonia. Terrorists clash with police and armed strike-breakers, coerce moderate trade unionists, hold up banks and businesses. Riff insurrection in Morocco.

1923
Spanish government discredited by failure to assert authority at home and abroad. General Primo de Rivera establishes military dictatorship.

1923–30
Primo de Rivera governs Spain with support of most of middle class and acquiescence of King Alfonso XIII. Wins cooperation of socialist-controlled General Workers' Union (U.G.T.). Socialist leader Francisco Largo Caballero a Councillor of State.

1926
Spain makes treaty of friendship with Italy.

1929–30
Economic recession and slow progress towards restoration of representative institutions gradually undermine confidence in Primo de Rivera. King accepts his resignation (1930) but can find no dictator or party government capable of replacing him.

1931
Most large towns return Republican councillors at municipal elections. King goes into voluntary exile. Spain becomes constitutional republic with Republican government responsible to Cortes dominated by socialists, radicals and radical socialists. Largo Caballero Minister of Labour. Manuel Azaña y Diaz, left-wing Republican Prime Minister, promises secularization of education and other reforms.

1932
Azaña antagonizes Right by anti-clericalism, disappoints Left by cautious attitude to agrarian reform. José Antonio Primo de Rivera, son of former dictator, founds anti-Marxist Falange Española.

1933
General election precipitated by constitutional crisis shifts power to Right and Centre.

1934
U.G.T., C.N.T. and communist party sponsor insurrection, which reaches serious proportions only in Asturias and Catalonia. Catalan autonomists proclaim existence of 'Catalan state within the Spanish Federal Republic'. Government uses Moroccan troops to restore order. About 20,000 militants arrested.

1934–5
President Alcalá Zamora, former liberal Republican politician, invokes presidential powers to enforce changes in Cabinet and prevent conservatives from using electoral advantage to block reforms. Big increase

in membership of communist party. Parties of Left agree to form Popular Front on lines recommended by Comintern.

1936

January

President dissolves Cortes in belief that general election will give moderates decisive victory.

February

General election. Popular Front wins slightly more than 200 seats out of total of 473 at first ballot. Electoral system calls for second ballot. Government resigns. Second ballot held at end of month under auspices of left-wing government headed by Azaña. Some evidence of intimidation of voters.

February–July

Popular Front government declares amnesty for militants jailed in 1934 and reinstates officials dismissed for complicity in insurrection. Strikes, armed clashes between Leftist and Rightist mobs, political assassinations, burning of barns and churches and murder of priests and nuns bring Spain to verge of civil war. Unemployment, unfavourable trade balance and withdrawal of foreign capital threaten economic collapse.

March

After scrutiny of votes cast at second ballot, Credentials Committee of Cortes declares 271 seats won by Popular Front. Chairman of Credentials Committee afterwards resigns, alleging fraud.

April–May

Government deposes Zamora. Nearly two-thirds of registered voters withhold votes at presidential election. Azaña declared elected.

12–13 July

Outrages by extremists of Left and Right culminate in shooting of police lieutenant and murder by uniformed men from police headquarters of José Calvo Sotelo, monarchist spokesman denounced by communist deputy Dolores Ibarruri ('La Pasionaria').

17 July
Army officers launch rebellion in Morocco.

18 July
Rebellion spreads to mainland. Rebels led by General Emilio Mola.

18–19 July
Azaña appoints new government headed by Diego Martínez Barrio, Speaker of Cortes and former leader of Republican Union Party.

19 July
Violent demonstrations against Barrio government. Mola rejects Barrio's offer of ceasefire, to be followed by formation of national government representing all major parties except communists. Left-wing government succeeds Barrio government and orders arming of revolutionary organizations.

20 July
Police and armed Leftists storm Montaña infantry barracks in Madrid and massacre rebel officers. Summary execution of prisoners soon becomes common practice on both sides.

20–31 July
Rebellion escalates into civil war between republicans and Nationalists. Nationalists overrun Morocco and capture Seville, Cordoba and much of northern Spain. Republicans hold Basque provinces, Madrid, Barcelona and most of south.

26 July
Léon Blum, Socialist Prime Minister in French Popular Front government elected May, announces France cannot intervene in Spanish Civil War. Comintern decides in principle to raise international force of communist volunteers for service in Spain. Hitler promises to send ammunition and limited numbers of aircraft to Nationalist Spain.

27 July
Mussolini makes similar promise.

2–4 August
French government proposes formal agreement between Britain, France and Italy not to intervene in Spain. French aircraft and volunteer airmen bound for Republican Spain begin to cross Pyrenees. Thirty-eight aircraft sent by 9 August, another fifty-six by 14 October. German transport aircraft carry rebel officers, and shortly afterwards begin to ferry Nationalist troops, from Morocco to Spain.

6 August
British and French governments submit draft non-intervention agreement to European powers.

14 August
Nationalists take Badajoz.

19 August
Anthony Eden, British Foreign Secretary, announces embargo on supply of arms to Spain. Tells representatives of Labour opposition there is no truth in rumour that Blum's announcement of 26 July was inspired by British.

21 August
Italy accepts non-intervention agreement but makes reservations about volunteers and financial support.

23 August
Soviet Union accepts non-intervention agreement. Small consignment of Soviet aircraft, with crews, said afterwards to have left Odessa for Republican Spain 23 July.

24 August
Germany accepts non-intervention agreement.

26 August
Alexander Orlov, of Soviet secret police, appointed adviser to Spanish Republican government on intelligence, counter-intelligence and guerilla warfare.

4 September
Largo Caballero heads new Republican Cabinet of five socialists, two communists, one crypto-communist, four Republicans of the Left and one Basque separatist.

5 September
Nationalists capture Irun.

13 September
Nationalists capture San Sebastian.

27 September
Nationalists capture Toledo.

October
Russian advisers supervise reorganization of Spanish Republican People's Army in brigade groups. Political commissars attached to all units from company level upwards. Soviet tanks and aircraft, with crews, reach Republicans in substantial numbers.

1 October
General San Miguel Cabanellas, Head of Provisional Junta in Nationalist Spain, appoints General Francisco Franco y Bahamonde generalissimo of armed forces and head of state.

22–5 October
Three-quarters of Spain's gold reserves shipped to Soviet Union on orders of Juan Negrín, Finance Minister in Largo Caballero government.

November
International Brigades, recruited by communist organizers in some twenty-five countries, begin to join Republican forces. Condor Legion, formed by Luftwaffe with initial establishment of 200 bomber, fighter, reconnaissance and transport aircraft, supplemented by anti-aircraft batteries, begins operations against Republican ports of supply. Soon turns, at Franco's request, to tactical support for troops. Air raids on Madrid. Republicans beat off attacks by Nationalist land forces.

4–6 November
Nationalist forces reach outskirts of Madrid.

6 November
Republican government leaves Madrid for Valencia.

December
Republicans repel further attacks on Madrid. Street fighting between C.N.T. and communists.

1937
6–28 February
Pre-emptive attack by Nationalists forestalls attempt by Republicans to concentrate forces for counter-offensive south of Madrid.

8 February
Capture of Malaga by Italian volunteers and other Nationalist forces shakes confidence in Republican leadership.

3–12 March
C.N.T. and Workers' Marxist Unification Party (POUM) in Catalonia disobey orders from central and regional governments requiring political and syndical organizations to surrender arms.

20–3 March
Battle of Guadalajara. Republicans inflict major setback on Italians by halting and dispersing force advancing on Madrid. Wet airfields without concrete runways prevent Condor Legion from using technique of close cooperation between ground and air tried out with conspicuous success in recent weeks.

26 March
C.N.T. representatives walk out of Catalan regional government.

19 April
Franco issues decree welding political organizations into single political authority and para-military organizations into national militia responsible to army. Principal organs of government to be head of state,

secretariat or Political Junta, National Council. National Council to consider questions remitted to it by head of state.

23 April
Largo Caballero dissolves communist-dominated Madrid Defence Junta.

26 April
Guernica laid waste, according to *prima facie* evidence, by bombing. Republicans allege intentional destruction of Basque religious capital by German bombers. Nationalist spokesmen attribute damage largely to blowing of demolition charges by Republicans. Luftwaffe officers say later report of devastation of Guernica came as complete surprise to them, and in any case Condor Legion's relatively small bomber and ground-attack forces not capable of destroying whole town.

27 April
Catalan regional government gives C.N.T. and POUM forty-eight hours to hand over weapons.

30 April–6 May
Street fighting in Barcelona. C.N.T. leaders negotiate ceasefire with central government.

15 May
Largo Caballero resigns premiership after rejecting communist demands for more rigorous control and sterner methods of repression by central government.

17 May
Comintern nominates Juan Negrín to head government dedicated to victory at any cost.

16 June
POUM dissolved and leaders arrested. Anti-Stalinist leader Andrés Nin tortured and executed by agents of Soviet secret police.

19 June
Nationalists capture Bilbao.

June–July
Soviet Union adopts policy of enabling Republicans to postpone defeat for as long as possible rather than helping them to gain outright victory. Recruiting for International Brigades dwindles.

5–28 July
Republicans attempt major offensive at Brunete but achieve little against better led and more mobile Nationalist forces with strong air support.

August
Unidentified aircraft and submarines attack merchant vessels in Mediterranean. Italian aircraft shadow British ships.

26 August
Nationalists capture Santander.

2 September
Italian submarine *Iride* makes unsuccessful attack on British destroyer *Havock*. British tanker S.S. *Woodford* reported sunk off south-east Spain at cost of one killed and six injured.

10–11 September
Nyon Conference. Nine European powers agree warships to patrol Mediterranean with orders to sink any submarine seen attacking a non-Spanish ship or suspected on good grounds of just having attacked one. Germany and Italy invited but do not attend.

14 September
Nyon agreement signed. No further acts of piracy in Mediterranean.

17 October
Largo Caballero addresses large audience in Madrid. Attacks policy of Negrín government from standpoint of loyal but highly critical observer. Denounces attempts by enemies to use power of state to oust him from U.G.T.

20 October
Nationalists capture Gijon.

21 October
Largo Caballero stopped by police on way to make speech at Alicante and placed under surveillance.

31 October
Republican government moves to Barcelona.

15–22 December
Republicans go over to offensive at Teruel with object of averting renewed threat to Madrid. Teruel surrounded.

1938
7–8 January
Republicans capture Teruel.

5–22 February
Nationalist counter-offensive. Teruel recaptured.

19 February
Anthony Eden resigns from Chamberlain government after failing to convince Chamberlain that withdrawal of some, at least, of Italian volunteers in Spain should precede formal talks with Italy about other matters.

March
Nationalists begin rapid advance with tanks and motorized infantry from Aragon towards Mediterranean. Half distance to sea covered between 9 and 15 March.

March–April
Frontier between France and Spain reopened for limited period during lifetime of Blum's second government. Republicans receive supplies from France and Soviet Union.

8 April
Indalecio Prieto y Tuero, socialist Minister of Defence in Negrín government, dismissed after protesting against attempt by communists to brand him as defeatist.

15 April
Nationalists reach Mediterranean at Vinaroz. Nearly 200,000 Republican troops in Catalonia cut off, except by sea and air, from more than twice as many in New Castile and Murcia. Republicans short of rifles and machine-guns and weakened by combat losses, desertions and execution of men accused of wishing to go over to the enemy.

30 April
Soviet figures show 31,237 recruits enrolled in International Brigades since recruiting began; 11,156 still serving, 4,575 killed up to 30 March.

April–May
Republicans call up nearly 200,000 men, open new training centres, reorganize troops on both flanks of Nationalist corridor.

June–July
Nationalists make unsuccessful attempt to capture Valencia by pushing south from corridor. German Ambassador, Moscow, reports (5 July) Soviet government no longer expects Republicans to win and thinks steps should be taken to reconcile public opinion to idea of negotiated peace. European powers accept plan for general withdrawal of volunteers and granting of belligerent rights to both sides. Only partial withdrawals follow.

July–August
Republicans cross Ebro and establish up to 50,000 troops in bridgeheads on right bank.

August
Basque and Catalan autonomist ministers resign from Negrín government. Catalanists discuss chances of making separate peace.

August-November
Franco suspends attempt to reach Valencia and uses small bodies of men, with strong air and artillery support, to pinch out Ebro bridgeheads. All surviving Republican troops back on left bank by 15 November.

December
Nationalists begin advance on Barcelona. Republican troops and civilians on short rations, though better fed in Catalonia than elsewhere. Appeal for volunteers to build fortifications and call-up of men up to age of forty-five in Catalonia yield meagre results.

1939
January
Basque and Catalan autonomist ministers rejoin Negrín government. Nationalist advance not effectively opposed. Barcelona surrenders 26 January.

February
Nationalists occupy whole of Catalonia. Azaña goes into exile in France 7 February, resigns presidency 24 February. Armed resistance in Catalonia ends 9 February. Large numbers of Republican troops retreat across frontier and are disarmed and herded into improvised camps by French authorities. Nationalist records show approximately 60,000 prisoners taken and 209,000 troops driven into exile. Negrín makes last of series of attempts to negotiate peace without reprisals.

26 February
Negrín calls meeting of military leaders at Albacete. Says large quantities of equipment and supplies about to arrive from Soviet Union. People's Army to make last stand at Cartagena naval base. Nearly 400,000 troops still nominally under arms in remaining Leftist zone, but only communists show any eagerness to continue the struggle.

4 March
Negrín assigns defence of key positions to communist military leaders. Commands given to or already held by communists include garrison of Cartagena, forces in Murcia, three out of four corps in Madrid area, most remaining armoured formations and reserve divisions.

5–12 March
Colonel Segismundo Casado, local commander in Madrid, leads rebellion against Negrín government, alleging government dominated by communists and communist takeover imminent. Sets up National

Defence Council. Comintern instructs Spanish communists to crush rebellion. Soviet officials depart in haste. Negrín takes refuge in France. Casado, reinforced by non-communist troops from outside Madrid, gains upper hand after week of fighting in which 2,000 killed. Julián Besteiro, distinguished socialist intellectual and member of National Defence Council, writes memorandum castigating folly of Spanish Left in following Stalinist line. He urges Republicans to cooperate with Nationalists in rebuilding Spain at end of war.

23 March
Casado's emissaries arrive Burgos with instructions to ask for terms. Franco demands surrender of Republican Air Force by 25 March and rest of armed forces by 27 March.

25 March
Franco breaks off negotiations on ground that Republican Air Force has not surrendered.

27 March
National Defence Council holds last meeting. Bands of young men appear in streets of Madrid and Valencia displaying Nationalist emblems and chanting Franco's name.

28 March
Nationalist forces enter Madrid.

29 March
Members of National Defence Council are able to leave Spain without molestation, but Besteiro refuses to go.

1939–40
Franco establishes anti-Marxist but not markedly pro-German or pro-Italian dictatorship buttressed by strong ties with church and army. Luis Araquistain, exiled former adherent of revolutionary wing of socialist party, foresees deal between Stalin and Hitler. Wholesale purge of wartime supporters of Republic by imprisonment, execution or dismissal from government posts. Besteiro sentenced to thirty years' imprisonment and dies in prison.

I

Reflection and Reinterpretation

HUGH THOMAS
CLAUD COCKBURN
BRIAN CROZIER
PETER KEMP

Hugh Thomas

At the time, the Spanish Civil War seemed, at least to the rest of the world, to be a struggle between Catholicism and atheism, between democracy and fascism, between revolution and reaction. There was no end to the different interpretations which could be given to it. Now, however, the picture is different. Time gives a different focus to everything. And it gives a different focus in 1975 from the one it gave in, say, 1960. Take a representative example. In the thirties, both the Spaniards and those foreigners who took part in the struggle were concerned with the international implications of the fighting. The Left saw themselves engaged in a battle against international fascism; the Right saw the fighting as part of the resistance to world communism.

Later, when the Civil War began to be treated historically, people emphasized the Spanish nature of the war. There might have been some contact between monarchists and Mussolini. There might have been a powerful Comintern delegation in Spain before the Civil War. But the causes of the war were to be found in Spanish history. Had not Spain gone to war over regional matters twice at least during the nineteenth century? Was not the fighting in Barcelona in the early twenties a rehearsal for the final class struggle? Finally, when it came to the war itself, were not the International Brigades only a small percentage of the Republican forces? Was not Republican disunity a powerful cause of the defeat?

Now, in 1976, it seems that the pendulum is swinging back. Recent historians have emphasized the importance not so much of men as of weapons, and weapon systems. How could the ordinary Spanish Republican cope with the 88-millimetre gun, afterwards so famous as an anti-tank gun, though used in Spain against aircraft? The Junkers 52 and Messerschmitt 109 aeroplanes, the Ansaldo–Fiat and Panzer mark 1 tanks also made their *débuts* in action in the Civil War in Spain. So too did such devilish contrivances as the Degtyarev machine-gun, the T–26 tank and the I–15 and I–16 fighters. About 2,000 foreign aircraft carried out sorties in action in Spain, and 1,000 tanks of foreign origin gave support to infantry, while a vast number of tactical innovations were worked out: 'the European Aldershot', as the German tank commander, General von Thoma, described the Civil War. Certainly many very advanced weapons were tried out between 1936 and 1939 in Europe's most technologically backward country. The technologically revolutionary side of the war was made even more obvious by the use of radio, the telephone and the news telegram.

But even more evidently international or continent-wide in its implications was the fact that the Spanish war obviously presented a Spanish version of many European stresses and strains. Although nationalist by definition, European fascism had many points in common wherever it appeared; and, even though the Spanish fascist party itself, the Falange, was relatively small before the Civil War began, many of the other right-wing attitudes which led to the formation of the national coalition in the Civil War bear a direct relation to similar attitudes in France, Italy or Germany.

This leads to a first general question in a contemporary reconsideration of the character of the Civil War: where does it stand in relation to Spain's modern development generally? And to this question, it may be added, a different answer must obviously be given after forty years of the Franco regime from any that could have been provided immediately after the war had ended, or even from the tentative answers of ten or twenty years ago.

Now in 1976 the Spanish Civil War seems, despite the emergence into Spanish life of a generation which was not specifically touched by it, to have constituted the most acute period of the modern Spanish political crisis which is still continuing today. That is, it marks neither the end nor the beginning of an era but rather lies about halfway between the present (another time of uncertainty) and the first moment when Spain's modern political problems were overtly posed, at the time of the First World War. At that time, during a period of high inflation, the working class in Andalusia were brought to a high pitch of expectation by the Russian Revolution. In Barcelona, the syndicalist-inspired workers in the textile mills similarly believed that their great opportunity had come. Catalan industrialists were divided as to whether or not they should embrace the idea of full independence for Catalonia. The army was also divided, in particular between those officers (*africanistas*) who had been active in fighting a rearguard action to preserve or extend Spanish influence in Morocco, and those stay-at-home officers (*peninsulares*) who resented the king's favouring of the *africanistas* with promotions and increased salaries.

Other problems in Spain were due to the divisions caused by the world war itself, in which the upper classes as a rule were friendly towards Germany, while the lower classes were mostly friendly towards the democracies. The complexity of the Spanish situation was compounded by differences of a mortal kind between the two main working class organizations of protest, the anarchists and the socialists, and by the dominant but much criticized position of the Church as the determining institution in Spain's educational and cultural life. Further problems were caused by nationalist stirrings both in the Basque country and in Galicia along the lines of those already evident for two generations in Catalonia.

All the problems at stake in the Civil War were thus essentially present twenty years before it broke out as a major conflict. Some might say that the Civil War simply represents the time when the Spanish conflicts, by an unhappy juxtaposition of international accidents, were rendered international in character. Certainly, they were not a matter of great international interest either before or since.

But we have to go even further back if we are to gain a genuine historical prospective on the Civil War. The Spanish nineteenth century was a time of extreme confusion. During the period of the restoration monarchy between 1875 and 1923 a serious effort was made to introduce a constitutional system. This failed partly because of the Moroccan wars, partly because of the Catalan problem, partly because of the anarchist character of the largest working class movement. Also, the type of democracy introduced was fairly corrupt, being based on local bosses in most of the country areas, and having little resilience after the murder of its chief initiator, the anglophile historian Cánovas. During the First World War, as has been seen, all the nation's troubles came to a head almost as sharply as they did in the belligerent countries. But in the end a socialist general strike was shot down by the army, a military expedition under General Barrera restored order in Andalusia, and another general, with a reputation for brutality in Morocco, Martínez Anido, did the same, though with great difficulty and at the cost of over 1,000 dead, in Barcelona. These two generals paved the way for a military *coup d'état* by another and more popular general, Primo de Rivera, in 1923.

Now in these events one can see very vividly the origins of Franco's regime, which has lasted for such a surprisingly long time since the Civil War ended: a revolutionary situation was brought under control by right-wing army officers, acting in the twenties, as in the thirties, as a kind of front for those forces of old Spain (Church, landowners, middle class) who were frightened by the revolutionary challenge from the Left.

Primo de Rivera's regime lasted until 1930, when another less effective officer took over for one year only. Then the officers and their incompletely realized plans were swept away after a large anti-monarchist vote in the municipal elections of April 1931. The king also himself was forced to withdraw and leave the country, and a Republican regime was introduced. For two years it attempted a wide range of progressive reforms – in Catalonia, in the Church, in the army, in education and on the land. The progressive politicians who introduced these plans had a large majority in the new parliament and underestimated the opposition which they might arouse. The Right, stunned by the demise of the dictatorship and the disappearance of the king, quickly recovered their coherence and energy in opposition to the government's somewhat hasty anti-clerical legislation. The government antagonized the forces of traditional Spain without satisfying those of the Left. Internal quarrels within the Republican camp caused a breakdown of the government and the calling of new elections (in 1933) long before they were due.

As it happened, those two years following the elections of April 1931 were the only ones in modern Spanish history when there has been a progressive government of a classic liberal type. For the new elections brought in a right-wing and centre majority. The socialists, largely because they saw their own country through the eyes of Europe as a whole, interpreted the (1934) entry into the government of three members of the newly formed Catholic Action Party as a fascist challenge. This took place at the end of a summer during which both ends of the Spanish political spectrum had been moving headily and fast towards their respective extremes. An agricultural strike, for example, in the course of the summer had been put down very fiercely, while several fringe parties, such as the small group of communists, the Carlists and the fascists of the Falange, had begun to organize military training. The subsequent revolution in October 1934 also implicated the Catalan separatist movement, the leader of whose autonomous government took a step towards complete independence by proclaiming the independence of the Catalan state within a Spanish federation.

The revolution failed everywhere, except in Asturias where the miners of the region held out against the army for several weeks. They were eventually crushed, though only after the Foreign Legion and Moroccan troops had been brought over from North Africa. Hundreds were killed, thousands imprisoned.

This was a victory for the Right and the Centre. But they could not agree among themselves any more than the Left had been able to two years before. Once again, there were new elections. These were held in February 1936 and gave a narrow minority to the Left, whose right wing, consisting of liberal professors and lawyers, formed a weak government which soon showed that it was quite incapable of maintaining itself against threats from Left and Right. On the Left, farms were occupied by the peasants, jobs and better wages were gained by intimidation and it was loudly proclaimed that revolution was only just round the corner. Even the hitherto reformist socialist party seemed to have become convinced that the millenium was at hand. On the Right, the fascist party (Falange) grew quickly, army officers plotted with bankers and monarchists, murders in the streets were an everyday occurrence. The months between the February elections and the outbreak of Civil War proper have been called the 'little civil war'. Certainly it is hard to maintain that the country was at peace.

In July, after many false alarms, the right-wing army officers staged their *coup d'état* and captured between a third and a half of Spain very quickly, including Morocco, the Canary Islands and most of the Balearics. But they did not win Madrid or Barcelona. The Civil War proper thus began, and both sides were appealing for foreign assistance before a week was out.

Left: King Alfonso XIII, who went into voluntary exile in 1931 with (*below*): General Primo de Rivera, who ruled Spain with his acquiescence

Above: A patrol on guard in Barcelona. *Below:* Civil guards, awaiting developments in a Madrid street

Above: Rioting in Madrid in April 1931, following the premature report of the abdication of King Alfonso. *Below:* A lorry load of students during their triumphal procession through Madrid, April 1931

Colonel Macía signs the proclamation of the Republic at Barcelona, 17 April 1931

Young fascists march through the buildings of the Barcelona Exhibition of 1931

The first elections under the new Spanish Republic in Madrid. Enthusiasts for the Republican cause in Spain canvassing

Civil guards of the government forces in action in the battle for Guadarrama, 3 August 1936

Government troops leave Madrid for Valencia, 5 August 1936

Government troops exultant after their victory in the battle of León, 5 August 1936

Government militiamen firing at rebels, 22 August 1936

Franco dines close to the battle line, February 1936

A woman member of the government forces helps two militiamen to hold a high position on the Aragon front, September 1936

A Nationalist cavalry column advances on a government position in the Albocacér sector, Province of Castellon

Franco's victory, after 1,000 days of war, was due to four main causes. First, although the army was divided by the rising, he had on his side the best and most experienced of the Spanish officers, in particular those who had done well ten years before in Morocco. Secondly, Franco, though by no means the senior officer at the beginning, managed to establish a real political unity on the Nationalist side whereas, among the Republicans, liberals, socialists, communists and anarchists were in constant conflict – sometimes, as in May 1937 and March 1939, even in open and physical confrontations. Thirdly, the assistance which the Nationalists got from Germany and Italy was on balance better and better used than anything which the Republic got from Russia or elsewhere on the free arms market. Here the amount of material was probably less important than its quality. Both sides were able to draw from two of the most modern arms industries, and Russia may even have sent as much war material as Italy and Germany did; the figures are not easy to disentangle because of artificial rates of exchange. In addition, the Nationalists got a regular supply of oil and some other goods from the U.S.A.; the Republic got their fuel either from Asturias (while they held it), or from Britain or Russia. Fourthly, the Nationalists inaugurated a fairly successful counter-revolution with many new features successfully introduced from Germany and Italy, and this brought the Spanish middle classes into willing cooperation with a military government which was originally not of its choice.

Victory left Franco in a position of supreme power which he retained until the 1970s. He skilfully manipulated the middle class forces which supported him, at one moment appearing to favour the Falange, at another the survivors of Catholic Action. The army always provided his chief support, but very few people had high positions under Franco who had any position at all in the right-wing governments of the early Republican years. In the immediate postwar period, old allies of Primo de Rivera came to the fore, but later the typical minister has been an opportunistic 'Francoist'.

Franco's regime has been unpopular abroad during much of its long period in power chiefly because of the brutal repression which it introduced from the beginning in the various territories where it was immediately victorious, and afterwards in the rest of Spain. It has, however, had two considerable successes: one in foreign policy, in that Franco managed to avoid being drawn into the world war despite his Civil War alliance with Germany and Italy, and subsequently succeeded in becoming an ally of the U.S.A. during the Cold War. The second achievement was to preside over the Spanish economic miracle of the 1960s which transformed the Spanish economy from a primarily agrarian one to one which was increasingly industrialized. Enormous new revenues were also coming in from tourism and the export of Spanish labour to other parts of Western Europe. But though the social structure has been transformed, there has been no recovery of the liberal freedoms which existed during the Republic and, in a slightly less open manner, before the dictatorship of Primo de Rivera. Indeed, from the angle of 1976 it seems that the emergence of Spain during the twentieth century has been conducted entirely by the authoritarian Right, the only exception being during the first two years of the Republic.

The last colony of the Spanish American empire was lost in 1898. That year seemed the nadir of Spain's fortunes. In fact, it marked the beginning of a recovery. The early part of the twentieth century was a time of very great artistic and intellectual vigour in Spain. This period reached its peak during the time of the Republic, Lorca being the best known name in literature, Picasso in painting. Spain certainly seemed to be coming out of its decline. After the Civil War, virtually an entire generation of intellectuals and artists went into exile, but in the 1960s this recovery was resumed, and it seems likely that Spain by the eighties will be one of the foremost countries of Europe intellectually – perhaps the foremost. From that angle, the Civil War will seem a severe interruption but by no means the end of an epoch and a process.

This intellectual recovery was matched, as might be expected, to the country's economic performance. The modernization of Spain began in the early part of the century, was given a new impulsion by the First World War, went ahead further during the dictatorship of the twenties but fell back severely during the thirties. The Civil War was a further tremendous setback and Spain's post-Civil War period was made all the more difficult in that it coincided with the Second World War. Afterwards, Spain was not included in the countries which received Marshall Aid. In 1953, Spain was still at the reduced level of industrial manufacture into which she had subsided in 1935. By the end of the fifties, however, the figures attained during Primo de

Rivera's dictatorship had been equalled, and by the end of the sixties they had been far exceeded.

The failure of the Republic of the 1930s was partly due to economic incompetence, but was more so to complex political causes. These took the form, as Raymond Carr has pointed out, of an increasing politicization of Spanish society, with the lead increasingly taken by the two extremes. The Republic was established during the world depression, and gradually the economy recovered slightly, as most economies did during the 1930s. Still, the economic performance of a country just before a catastrophe cannot be wholly irrelevant. The depression's most obvious manifestation in Spain as elsewhere was rising unemployment. In Spain at this time there was no unemployment relief. By the spring of 1936, the total unemployed must have numbered about 700,000, out of a total labour force of not much more than eight or nine million. Huge numbers of these unemployed joined one or other of the private armies of bodyguards, 'militants', messengers and others which were increasingly maintained by the political parties. Often they could not be paid, but at least they could be given a gun. The existence of these large politically conscious unemployed groups, with many more under-employed for much of the year, was probably one of the main reasons for the war.

The politics of the war itself are a fairly baffling maze. At first sight, there seem to be definite similarities between what happened on the two sides. Thus the first stage of the war was that of the 'cantonalization' of Spain, Left and Right, accompanied everywhere by executions, random shootings and confiscations. In that first stage, the cantonalization was more pronounced on the side of the Republic than that of the rebels: how many small states there seemed to be in the summer of 1936, each seeking its own idiosyncratic way to liberty! Slowly, by the autumn, authority was gaining the upper hand on both sides. By the winter, the army in the rebel zone had been concentrated under the command of Franco, though his authority was somewhat limited by the initiative of such local bosses as Queipo de Llano in Seville and Cañizares in Badajoz. In the Republican zone, governmental authority was also slowly restored, although the communist-dominated Council of Defence in Madrid, the anarchist council of Aragon, the socialist defence committee in Malaga, to mention only a few of the almost independent bodies, were still virtually autonomous.

In Barcelona power was still shared between the Catalan government and the anarchists, while the communists sought to reinforce the first against the second and then to bring all the Catalans into control by the central power.

During the spring of 1937, both sides also had difficulties with their extremist minorities. In April Franco staged a virtual *coup d'état* over Hedilla and the large army of ambitious fascists, and then united the Carlists, the fascists and all other extant parties into a single 'movement' under his leadership. Henceforth, apart from some grumbles by outspoken generals such as Yagüe, Franco had no difficulties of a political nature until the end of the war – indeed until much later than that.

The right-wing socialists, allied with the communists, made a similar capture of the Republican state in May 1937, after the outbreak of the fighting in Barcelona so vividly described by Orwell, which isolated the left-wing socialists (headed by the ex-Prime Minister Largo Caballero) and the anarchists. The POUM, the small sect of revolutionary but anti-Stalinist communists who included Trotsky's ex-secretary Nin, were actually banned, their leaders being gaoled or, in the case of Nin and some other lesser people, murdered by communists. Thereafter, the two sides were both led by men who had played only a minor part in the life of the Republic; Franco, who had been army chief of staff during the Asturias revolution, and Negrín, professor of physiology, who had done much to organize the establishment of the new university city just outside Madrid, in which some of the bitterest fighting had taken place during the winter of 1936. Neither perhaps would have come to the top in peacetime politics, for both were poor speakers and the Spanish parliament had placed a premium on the spoken word. But both were realists, and both made numerous if reluctant concessions to their external allies – Germany and Italy, in Franco's case, Russia, in the case of Negrín.

The economies of the two zones also bore a certain resemblance to each other by the end of the war. The Republican government had brought all collective experiments to an end, had greatly increased the role of the central state delegate even in anarchist factories, and had sought to bring all agricultural marketing under the control of the Ministry of Agriculture, whether or not the produce derived from a private farm or from a collective (of which many had been formed during the days which Malraux wrote of as 'l'illusion lyrique'). The Republican administration also attempted, without much success, to encourage the return of foreign capitalists who had fled during the early days. On the Nationalist side, there was a similar absence of ideology by the end of the war. Verbal concessions had been made to fascism and land confiscated under the Republic had been handed back; but the regime, under German advice, practised the somewhat colourless war socialism of Germany during the First World War rather than any form of pure private enterprise.

But further points of comparison would be misleading. Franco's Spain was first and foremost a military zone. The subservience of everything to the army command was one reason why Franco was able to move his troops about from one front to another with such apparent ease. Negrín's Spain remained civilian, and its political contradictions were a continuous hindrance to effective decision-making even on military matters. Yet democratic procedure had vanished as soon as the war began. Between July 1936 and February 1939 the Cortes, for example, met five or six times only, and then simply to take note of perfunctory speeches by the government. The Republic permitted all the natural political intrigues of democracy but without any of its vital realities. The relations between military and civilian authority were never clear. True, the Republic built up an army, but officers never knew when some petty potentate would not interfere to damage the efficacy of their command. General Llano de la Encomienda, for example, was named commander-in-chief of the whole of the northern front, including the Basque country, Asturias and Santander. But not only did the Basque nationalist leader communicate regularly with the Republican Minister of Defence in Valencia (once causing the poor general to ask if the 'Army of the North' still existed) but Llano de la Encomienda had to put up with all the delays and inconveniences of different regional customs in the area of his command.

Again, these two huge armies, each almost a million strong, were utterly unlike each other both in tradition and in composition. The Nationalist army was quite free of politics, though everyone knew that General Kindelán and General Vigón, say, were monarchists, and General Yagüe a Falangist. The Republican army, on the other hand, was first of all divided between ex-regular officers and ex-militia officers – that is, men who had taken the lead in the early days of the militarized section of one or other of the working class units. The professional difference between these two groups was also conspicuous. General Menéndez, for example, said that, of the militia leaders beside him in the Battle of Brunete, not only was there only one (Modesto) who knew how to read a map, but the others (Lister, Campesino, Mera, etc.) did not even acknowledge the need to do so. Another anecdote is even more revealing: at the end of the Civil War, two ex-regular officers of the Republican side went to negotiate peace terms with Franco's men at Burgos airport. The atmosphere was understandably icy, but over lunch one of Franco's officers did say to one of the two Republicans that he could not understand how it was that he, an officer of the old school, could have brought himself to fight on the same side as such canaille. The Republican officer replied with dignity that if only people like himself had had their way in running the army they would have won.

Then, besides this difference of origins, there were also endless political difficulties between officers of both professional and militia origins: communist, anarchist and liberal affiliations in the army never vanished, and were constantly being revived, owing to the presence of a considerable number of Russian advisers who naturally favoured communist officers against the others. There was no hint of this sort of difficulty on the Nationalist side, though Franco certainly got on badly with some of the officers sent to him by the Germans and the Italians. (The worst such instance was his difficulty with General Roatta, the Italian commander-in-chief at the time of the Battle of Guadalajara.)

But the chief difference between the two camps in the Civil War was the solid fact of unity on the Nationalist side on all important issues, and the grumbling disputes which persisted throughout on the Republican side, in particular those between the communists and a variety of successive opponents.

At the beginning of the Civil War, the communists were much the smallest of the revolutionary parties in the Republic. They had about sixteen M.P.s out of 475 in the Cortes, of whom only one, the silver-tongued La Pasionaria, was at all well known. Still, they had a number of advantages. The first of these was their leadership in the cause of the Popular Front, which was a compelling international vision during the years before the Second World War. The communists also had many friends in the socialist party, particularly among the socialist youth, around the person of Largo Caballero, and in Catalonia. They also had at their service a powerful delegation from the Comintern.

The trajectory of the communist party is not altogether easy to follow but to do so is nevertheless to follow the political fortunes of the Republic in a very precise manner. Before the Civil War, the communists were apparently trying to press the socialist party leftwards in an authentically revolutionary manner. In this, they were very successful, helped in particular by the young socialists, who formally merged with the communist youth movement a few weeks before the war began. Santiago Carrillo, the socialist youth leader, has said recently, in his *Demain Espagne* (conversations with Régis Debray and Max Gallo) that he was attending meetings of the Communist Party Central Committee even before that (though he did not himself formally become a communist until November). The behaviour of the young socialist-communist activists before the war, combined with that of fellow-travellers high up in the socialist hierarchy (such as Alvarez de Vayo), was very destructive. One can only speculate as yet on the attitude of Comintern advisers, such as the Argentine-Italian Codovilla, who must have believed that genuine revolutionary possibilities were opening out in Spain in the early part of 1936. At that time his instructions were to stick to the international communist line of a Popular Front in cooperation with middle class democratic parties against fascism. In fact, he wished to present a civilized 'pragmatic' face to the world.

When the Civil War broke out, the communists were the most disciplined of the parties supporting the government and they vigorously defended the principle of state authority against the revolutionary innovations sought by the anarchists and some of the socialists. Within weeks, their growing numbers had made them indispensable. Also helpful were their propaganda skill, their superior military discipline and their political moderation. The hard-pressed central governments in both Madrid and Barcelona, liberal though they might have been in intention, turned to the communists in their efforts to restore their own authority at any moment of particular confusion. Within a month, the communists were the strongest influence within the previously socialist-dominated trade union, the U.G.T. in Catalonia – though this organization was very much smaller than the anarchists' C.N.T. The commitment of Russia to supply arms to the Republic, as well as a number of experienced soldiers as military advisers, not to speak of the Comintern's organization of the International Brigades, completed the communists' triumph. In September, two communists entered the coalition cabinet under Largo Caballero and others worked in other sections of the state hierarchy, particularly in the army. By the end of 1936, the communist party in Spain had swollen to 300,000 members, according to their own count, of whom half were apparently in the army and another third, surprisingly, were private peasants (many such small farmers had drawn towards the communists in order to escape having to join an anarchist collective). Other people, who would previously have been regarded as 'bourgeois', joined the communist party in droves: army officers, engineers, civil servants, shopkeepers – all joined without reading a word of Marx because they thought that the communists were the party of the future, because they knew Russia had the guns which they needed, and because of the communists' moderate policy on all social questions. Right-wing socialists even argued for a merger between their two parties with the object of crushing the extreme leftists.

This was a strange communist party. Its leaders might say that moderation was necessary for the duration of the war. Afterwards, they implied, they could set about the serious business of making the revolution. But many of their followers – perhaps a majority – were communists because they saw in that affiliation a means of defeating the revolution altogether. Hence the continuing sympathy felt for the party by high-minded men such as President Manuel Azaña, who was aghast at the outbreak of the war in the first place, and whose political programme, by early 1937, amounted to nothing more than survival and the preservation of some degree of state authority.

Perhaps this explains, in retrospect, the strangely complacent attitude of such men towards the whole policy of persecution which the Moscow-directed communists soon visited upon all who ventured to criticize their moderate line. The principal victims were Andrés Nin and the POUM. The persecution of the latter was simply an extension of the Moscow purges into Spain. There were the beginnings of a similar policy towards the anarchists also, but they were too strong and active to be completely crushed. By the end of 1937, however, there were an alarmingly large number of left-wing heretics in Republican gaols, and some International Brigade volunteers were going home disillusioned by communist dishonesty and power-seeking. In addition, some heretics were murdered, and infamous torture and interrogation chambers were set up in Barcelona and elsewhere, modelled on those of Moscow and staffed by people specially sent from Russia to carry on Stalin's vendettas in a Latin country. By this time Largo Caballero, disillusioned with the communists, had given way to the tactically agile realist, Negrín.

The last eighteen months of the war were dominated by an alliance between the right-wing socialists (Negrín and Prieto), the liberals (Azaña) and the communists. In the end, both Prieto and Azaña had followed Largo into total disillusionment with the communists, and only the communists and Negrín kept the war going, supported by a few other right-wing socialists. Otherwise, optimism was the only programme, and it was not an easy one to maintain in the face of continuous military defeats and a rapidly declining economy. (Inflation in the Spanish Republic was very severe: the general price index doubled between July 1936 and September 1937, and probably doubled again before the end of the war. This was caused by the diminished production of all major industrial plants during these years, the political confusion caused by so many ill-coordinated schemes for workers' control, and the loss of both markets and sources of raw materials for such industries as the Catalan textile factories.)

Nevertheless, the opposition within the Republic had one final card to play. After the collapse of Catalonia, the government returned to the central zone apparently determined to carry on the fight there. But disillusion was widespread. Liberals, anarchists and right-wing and left-wing socialists all banded together to support the ill-fated *coup d'état* of Colonel Casado in Madrid, directed against Negrín and the communist leaders, who now found themselves completely without support. Many of the army officers who had happily declared themselves communists in the great days of the defence of Madrid showed themselves to be fair-weather communists only. The suggestion that all should now collaborate on the programme of resistance *à l'outrance* was unpopular and seemed implausible when so many of those calling for resistance were making sure that they had passports and safe foreign havens. Meantime, Russian arms were getting through to Spain only with difficulty because of Italian activity in the Mediterranean and the French reluctance to quarrel with the British over the internationally agreed policy of non-intervention. After Munich, furthermore, there were many signs suggesting that Stalin was contemplating cutting his losses in Spain.

Colonel Casado's *coup d'état* was carried out with the specific intention of opening peace negotiations. But there were to be no negotiations, and the Republican army surrendered virtually unconditionally, with no guarantees against reprisals except in the case of a few officers who had assisted in the last-minute negotiations. The communist leaders left for abroad; many of their rank and file were handed over directly to Franco to be shot; they had been conveniently imprisoned by Casado while the war was still being fought.

On the Nationalist side, there was nothing like this *dégringolade*. The middle class rallied more and more round Franco, a leader whose relative youth commended him to young fascists, whose military success made him popular in the army, and whose solid middle class origins (his ancestors had been in naval administration for several generations) made him seem like a successful member of their own class to the bourgeoisie. The monarchists thought that Franco was a monarchist, since he had been a protégé of ex-King Alfonso and some of his speeches when commandant of the military academy at Saragossa had been irreproachably monarchist in tone. An active group of young Falangists also gave 'the crusade of liberation', as it was known, a patina of Mussolinian or Hitlerian culture, cutting out French words from menus, changing street names, ensuring that Republican leaders' birth certificates were removed from records, bullying people who spoke with a Catalan accent, and attempting to wipe out any recollection of decadent liberalism or even any memory connected with the French Revolution. Purges of civil servants, teachers and post office officials accompanied the more brutal repression. Writers and artists who had felt themselves slighted by the fashionable leftism in the arts and the universities during the Republic found good appointments in the purged university faculties or on new newspapers and tried to teach their readers to speak the 'language of empire'.

The Spanish Civil War casts a heavy shadow over modern Spain even though it ended forty years ago. I suspect that, as with modern Russia, modern Spaniards will not be able to face the future with confidence until the distressing lessons of the recent past have been properly learned.

Claud Cockburn

No one can possibly say what would have happened if something also had not happened instead. That sort of speculation is gossip. It differs from gossip, idle or otherwise, regarding contemporary goings on because chit-chat about what these or those people are allegedly up to now can occasionally be either verified or proved false. This consideration might, but seldom does, inhibit a lot of tittle-tattle, sometimes amusing sometimes positively furious, about events that never came to pass, so that you can often hear serious, even bitterly contentious, discussion about, for example, what would have happened had the Republicans won the Civil War in Spain.

Speculating thus, someone will opine that a Republican victory would have prevented the outbreak of the Second World War. How? Because it would have incalculably strengthened the Popular Front in France, compelled the French government to act effectively in the organization of collective security against Hitler, and in consequence caused the notoriously hesitant German General Staff to refuse its backing for Hitler's bellicose gambles. Also it would so mightily have encouraged the British Left that Neville Chamberlain would have been politically paralysed before he could fly to Munich, Czechoslovakia would not have been abandoned, and Europe would have been saved for peace and democracy.

Perhaps.

But another speculator, with a different hot-line to non-history, is nearly sure that a triumph of the Left in Spain would have thrown such a scare into the British and French upper and middle classes that they would have seen Hitler as their sole salvation from ruin, and established some form of fascism in Britain and France – and how would you have liked that?

The only certainty is that if the Civil War had ended otherwise, the subsequent history of Europe would have been incalculably different too. And that was among the facts which, being recognized at the time by all but the abnormally obtuse, seized the attention and stirred the passions of millions in Europe and the United States. They rightly saw in that war a climactic event of which the outcome was going to affect, and affect very soon, the lives of people a long way from the Iberian peninsula and previously more or less indifferent to its affairs.

Anyone who travelled back and forth in Republican territory during the war could observe the high degree – amazing and even alarming to some such travellers – to which the Spanish Republicans, from farm workers and peasants to the professional class and the intellectuals, were conscious of the wider implications of this geographically localized conflict.

One night in September 1936, in a dugout on a high ridge of the sierra north of Madrid, then the front line, a group of Spanish militiamen, some peasants, some industrial workers, were discussing the situation. Half a mile to the north-west, on the opposite ridge, a battalion of Moorish machine-gunners manned their blockhouses. To the south we could see a faint light in the sky, thrown up from the suburbs of Madrid, not yet blacked out. All day Italian Capronis had flown at a few hundred feet, back and forth along the ridge, dropping smallish bombs. All evening the Republican radio had been announcing either imaginary victories or 'rectifications of the line' – meaning defeats and retreats.

A militiaman, a mechanic from the city who had been a member of the armed forces for a fortnight, said: 'You understand I'm ready to die to save Madrid.' He waved his hand in the direction of the city. 'I'm ready to die to save democracy and civilization from fascism. But I'm damned if I'm going to die just to prevent a rectification of the line. And what I'd like to know is whether, supposing we and the rest of this regiment bugger off out of his bloody awful dugout before we get the shit blown out of us, that would be a betrayal of civilization or a rectification of the line?'

It seemed to me about as humanly sensible a question as I ever heard asked, and it was accepted as such by all present. There followed a long discussion of the world situation, in particular the attitudes of the British and the French. How might all this be affected for better or worse by the behaviour of the men in the bloody awful dugout? The consensus was that although withdrawal might constitute no more than a rectification of the line, there was a better than even chance that it could be the start of something disastrous for Madrid, for democracy, and for civilization. Naturally there were two or three who ventured to suggest we might run the risk and let civilization take care of itself while we retired to a deeper dugout on a less exposed ridge. Their feelings on the matter were strengthened by a suspicion that this particular defensive position had been chosen by the officer immediately in command not because it was the best position but because it was the worst. Their suspicions were justified. The officer, one of the few officers of the regular army who had appeared to remain loyal to the Republic, deserted to the fascists a few days later.

That treachery was a way of life among the regular officers, that the enemy were both better equipped and incomparably better trained than themselves, and that the French and British governments had cut off the arms supply to the Republic, were facts known to all. But the feeling of the majority in that dugout was that, things being what they were, they were proud, if not exactly happy, to be just where they were at just that time. They had, after all, volunteered not because they thought their government knew best what had to be done about fascism. They believed they knew best themselves.

That sort of discussion was going on all along the fighting fronts of the Republic and in the hinterland. It would be fatuous to suggest that most of those concerned were preoccupied or fuelled mainly by the notion that they were saving European civilization from the barbarians. They were, in the first instance, acting in simple self-defence. They had much experience of the Spanish ruling class, and thus a clear understanding of what would happen to the workers, peasants, professional people and intellectuals if the fascist attack led by General Franco were to succeed. Their trade unions and village committees and other protective organizations would be destroyed. Their wages and salaries would be pushed down to the poverty line and kept there for years to come. An illiterate peasant from north of Almeria said to me, 'If those people win, my children will never get an education either.'

But this natural instinct of self-defence against the enemy had, that year in Spain, two particular characteristics. Those people were not defending long established or traditional standards, rights and powers. The standards, rights and powers that they had were acquisitions recently gained, for the most part in the turmoil of the years just before and after the overthrow of the monarchy. And they had not been gained without struggle, suffering and setbacks in the face of powerful and savage attempts at repression. Secondly, and this was vital in their thinking, they saw themselves defending not only the novel and precarious present, but the potentially wonderful future. They were fighting to protect not only what they had but what they hoped for. The 150 days between the victory of the Popular Front in the February elections of 1936, and the military counter-attack in July, had indeed been, in Malraux's phrase, the days of hope. And, as General de Gaulle said to Malraux thirty-five years later: 'If what I had done had not carried hope within itself, how could I have done it? Action and hope are inseparable. It certainly seems that only human beings are capable of hope. And remember that in the individual, the end of hope is the beginning of death.'

The hopes of the Spaniards were modest or extravagant according to your assessment of what a human being may rightfully hope for.

During the sporadic struggles of the recent years they had often heard the slogan, voiced by La Pasionaria during the 1934 miners' revolt in the Asturias, 'It is better to die on your feet than live on your knees'. They believed that under the democratic government supposedly established by the February elections it might be possible to avoid having to choose one or other of these disagreeable alternatives. A person might be able to stand up on his two feet and live. They thought that democracy meant power for the people, and, with that power achieved at the ballot boxes, they believed they had ground upon which to build high hopes for the future of Spain.

For instance, the workers in the factories knew that Spain's industrial plant was among the most modern in Europe. The people who worked the plant lived poorly, on miserable wages. And often enough the only effective way to a wage rise appeared to be to call upon the able gunmen of the highly organized anarchist General Union of Workers, sometimes capable of terrorizing the industrialists into persuading the bankers – Spanish or foreign – who ultimately owned them into paying out. In this respect the anarchists frequently achieved good results. But in a democracy, it was imagined, it would be easier to ensure that the products of those fine factories would ensure high standards of living for the people who worked them. The market could be anywhere. But there was certainly a huge potential market right on the doorstep. Modern machinery and irrigation could make three blades of grass grow on the vast agricultural acreage of Spain where one had grown before. And for that, of course, democratic power would provide a fundamental reorganization of the system of land ownership. The enormous, ill-managed *latifundia*, largely owned and wasted by absentee landlords, would have to be taken over, redistributed and run for the benefit of the people who worked the fields and pastures.

In the light of what really happened to that democracy it is possible to see those hopes and expectations as having been absurd. But they were the hopes people had at the time, and to them they seemed both rational and worth fighting for. They were naive in the way the radicals of nineteenth-century Europe can be regarded, by embittered hindsight, as having been naive. They believed, for instance, that science, in the service of the people, could bring the good life and happiness to all labouring mankind.

But they read the newspapers, or, if illiterate, had the newspapers read aloud to them. They listened to innumerable orators. They knew a great deal about fascism in Italy and Germany. And they were not – at least for the most part – so naive as to suppose that the Spanish ruling class would quietly accept the verdict of the ballot box. Professor Laski said that the Gentlemen of England always play the game, but reserve the right to change the rules in the middle if they find they are losing. This was not a gibe fairly applicable to the Gentlemen of Spain. They had never made much serious pretence of playing the democratic game. Their behaviour was reminiscent rather of G. K. Chesterton's remark that 'the poor have sometimes objected to being badly governed. The rich have always objected to being governed at all.'

Most people were theoretically aware, or felt in their bones, that the Right would counter-attack. But, as some theologian has said, 'we can be said to believe something when we are prepared to act as though it were true'. And the Spanish Republicans did not act as though it were true that the counter-attack was imminent. The liberal leaders of the Popular Front could not act positively in that sense, because to do so would have involved recognizing and arming working class militias, and thus an unacceptable increase in anarchist and socialist power. The socialist leaders, on a strict diet of doctrinaire milk of the word, were afraid they would compromise themselves by too close an alliance with the bourgeois parties in face of the lowering enemy. They acted as though they believed themselves when they declared that the dictatorship of the proletariat would at some point succeed the Popular Front government, without considering the likelihood that they and the government would be destroyed together by the Right. The anarchists, equally hidebound by their own traditions, doctrines and theoretical aims, saw united action against the common enemy as a betrayal of those traditions, and, since it involved a strengthening of the state, a negation of those ultimate aims. The communists put the defence of the Republic against the enemy as the primary and essential point on the agenda. But at that time their numbers were very small, and their power almost negligible.

Against those who called for unity, it was argued, and by many sincerely believed, that these debilitating diversities and divisions were inherent in the nature of democracy itself; thus lethal intra-Republican conflicts could, properly regarded, be seen as proof that the Republic was an authentic democracy, entitled to put B.A.(Dem.) on its national card. Those who thus argued would have said, had the word been in vogue at the time, 'This is a pluralist society. Give us pluralism or give us death.' In the event, both they and 'pluralism' were given death.

The leaders of these divisive struggles for the most part conducted them under the umbrella of a fatal hallucination. Simply, they believed in forms of international solidarity which did not exist. The liberals thought that if it came to the worst, the British and French democracies would be on their side against fascist attack, not merely for ideological reasons but because they needed a democratic Spain in face of the German and Italian menace to themselves. The socialists, suspicious of the British Conservative government, thought that – again, if it came to the worst – the British Labour Party and the powerful trade union movement would nobly exert themselves on their behalf.

On the eve of the Civil War and immediately after the outbreak, I used to argue with such of the Republican leaders as I knew well that all this was an illusion. So far as the British government and the British Labour and trade union leadership were concerned, any government with a red tinge was leprous. They made clear that they considered me unduly cynical, lacking in patriotism and understanding of my fellow countrymen. They were thus astounded when, in the first week of August – a bare fortnight after the launching of Franco's attack – they learned that the British ambassador in Paris had officially warned the French government of what Britain would do if the French government failed to prohibit the export of war material of any kind to the Republic, even though the supply of these arms had already been contracted for. If the French allowed arms to cross the Pyrenees to the Republic, then Britain would repudiate its obligation (under the Treaty of Locarno) to come to the aid of France in case of war with Germany. In other words, if Hitler chose to regard the passage of arms from France to Spain as a *casus belli* and attacked France, the British would abandon France. The British threat was, of course, successful in throttling the arms supply. It was no comfort at all to have it proved that I was not so foolishly cynical as some members of the then Republican government thought me, and that I understood the real policy of the British government better than they did.

This did not prevent them believing that at least the British labour movement would back the Spanish workers now fully engaged in desperate struggle. In this matter, too, they were harshly disappointed.

In those days of isolation, when no reasonably cool-headed person would have bet on the chances of survival at less than 100–1 against, I was in a Madrid street watching a communist convoy leaving for the front, which was already unpleasantly close. A little way off could be seen the militia guarding the palace of the Duke of Alba. The palace, full of great pictures and other art treasures, had been opened as a museum of art, and was daily thronged. Given the disturbed state of the city, there was naturally fear lest hooligans, or possibly some organized gang of international picture thieves, might break in and steal. The only ruffians who did in fact attack the palace a little later were a couple of low-flying Italian bombers. It was believed in Madrid that the palace had been pinpointed in that way on the particular instructions of the Duke of Alba who, it was alleged, would rather see those art treasures destroyed than displayed to the vulgar. I have no idea whether this story was true or not. But the fact that it was immediately assumed to be true, and indeed the expected thing for the duke to do, was an indication of the kind of reputation the Gentlemen of Spain had made for themselves. They were, after all, in alliance with General Goering, who had notoriously remarked that when he heard the word 'culture' he reached for a gun.

At the back of the last lorry of the convoy, a young man jumped up from among the crowded huddle of his companions and addressed the heavens above. He wore factory worker's overalls, but on top of them a grotesquely ill-fitting regular army tunic. I recalled that some genius, brooding on the fact that the fascists shot most of their prisoners, had pointed out that killing of prisoners might perhaps be justified before some international court if those prisoners were in civilian clothes at the time. But, said this same genius, if our men were in uniform, it said in the Geneva Convention that shooting them was prohibited. The result was that the Republicans, who believed in conceptions of international law long since abandoned by the enemy, wasted a lot of time ransacking the quartermasters' stores of the regular army for bits and pieces of uniforms. I personally suffered from this absurdity because when I joined the Republican army and went up to fight with those people on the sierra, they fitted me out with a pair of cavalryman's breeches. Very fine, and if those Moors had taken a look at them they would have remembered the Geneva Convention and said, 'We cannot shoot this uniformed soldier.' Unfortunately the axiom in the Spanish army was that the taller a man is the fatter he must be. Being rather tall and thin, I was not suited by those breeches, and I had to tie them round my waist with a series of knotted handkerchiefs. One night, as I retreated at as fast a run as I could manage from advancing fascists, leaping from rock to rock of that sierran slope, the handkerchiefs unknotted themselves, and I, tackled low around the knees by the falling breeches, fell heels over head. I thought what a way to go, shot or bayoneted with your pants literally down. Luckily, what with the shock and the fear, I was stunned into total silence and immobility, and the Moors passed by and then returned to their positions. Hitching up my pants I returned zigzag to our lines. But the zigzag had been extensive and the sector I struck was manned by anarchists who had a mind to shoot me, on the ground that I was fighting with the next group along the sierra who were believed to be socialists and communists, and was in any case a British imperialist.

I told them, truthfully, that I was a Scotsman, born in Pekin China. After these circumstances had been discussed at length, there was a consensus against shooting me. All the same it had been a worrying night. I walked, cursing the Geneva Convention, through the sweet-smelling pinewoods and experienced, not for the first or last time, the exquisite happiness of not being dead.

The young man in the ill-fitting tunic, which was to afford him the full protection of the Geneva Convention, was armed with a First World War rifle, and a couple of locally manufactured hand-grenades which, as I had often had occasion to observe, might sometimes explode on target, but just as often in the hand of the thrower. You must cast your mind back to the days when even the primitive Molotov Cocktail, which today even small children in the streets of Belfast and other cities know how to operate, was a rarity.

I reflected that, given the forces against him – the Italian aeroplanes, the German aeroplanes, and the quantity of artillery and machine-guns supplied by Hitler and Mussolini – and the fact that he was going to be fighting against seasoned troops, having himself had less than ten days' training, that fine-looking young man was unlikely to live very long. But he was shouting at the sky in a tone of triumph and, at the conclusion of his address, he raised his voice to roar out with peculiar intensity the most familiar Republican slogan of that time: 'Viva la República! Viva Democracia! Viva Yo!'

For the first time it occurred to me as being significant that there was no way of fully translating that 'Viva Yo!' into any language known to me. A British soldier might certainly be thinking 'Long live Me!', but it would sound odd if he shouted it out. The French say 'Vive Bibi!' but it has a humorous, slightly self-mocking nuance. For the Spaniards it was a serious expression of what they were fighting for. Sapient liberal sociologists might have tried to demonstrate to that young communist soldier that it is really hopeless to suppose that it is possible to combine effective, disciplined collective action with full scope for the 'Yo'. He would have thought they were talking through the backs of their necks.

As the outlook for the Republic, democracy, and 'Yo' seemed to darken hopelessly, three developments began to change the shape of things. One was the rapid, though arduous and never quite complete, agreement among the Republican political factions to restrict their political feuding to areas where it would not impede the joint resistance to the fascist attack. The most important feature of this general agreement was that in practical, military terms, it implied acceptance of a unified command, the integration of the militias in a new Republican army, and the acceptance of forms of military discipline of a kind which in blither days had been repugnant to, in particular, the anarchists. The model for the new sort of Republican army had been established as early as mid-August, when the communists organized what was called the 5th Regiment, politically non-denominational, independent of the various militias, and accepting rigours of training and discipline unknown to the militias. These developments, under communist influence, were bitterly criticized by the same sort of people who, much later, sentimentalized about the 'little men in black pyjamas' in Vietnam and were bothered when the requirements of war changed the touching image.

The second revitalizing event was the arrival on the front of the first battalions of the International Brigade. Militarily, these anti-fascist fighters from all over Europe saved Madrid from Franco's first, seemingly irresistible attack. Morally, their impact was enormous. Those men were a living demonstration to the Spaniards that the solidarity of the working people of Europe against fascism was not, as they had been tempted to fear, a mere illusion.

The third thing that happened was the arrival, first in a trickle, very soon in a big stream, of Soviet planes, Soviet tanks, Soviet artillery, and Soviet technicians. Militarily, those armaments tilted towards something approaching equality the balance of weaponry on the fronts. Morally, the effect upon people who, week after week, had seen the Italian and German bombers going about their business with hardly any let or hindrance, and who knew that there was nothing serious in the way of arms to be expected from France, was incalculably profound. When they learned in the hardest possible way that their imagined allies, the Western democracies, had abandoned them, the Spaniards had said, 'But the Russians – the Russians will come.' And in the amazing dawn of one day in Madrid, as the Capronis and the Junkers lumbered confidently low over the city, fighter planes none of us had ever seen before came racing in out of the eastern sky. The bombers were shot down or fled, and the people rushed to the rooftops or into the streets dancing and cheering. The Russians had come.

I spent that day with my friend Michael Koltzov, who was foreign editor of *Pravda*. The reason why the foreign editor of the world's largest circulation newspaper was not sitting in Moscow foreign-editing, but instead sitting here in Madrid, or bouncing all over Republican Spain like an electrified ball, was that he had been chosen by the Politburo in the Kremlin as the man best suited to assess the true situation in Spain as it developed, to explain Soviet attitudes to Spanish ministers less formally and yet more impressively than the ambassador, and to convey the results of all this activity to Moscow. He had, in fact, a direct line from his room in the Palace Hotel, Madrid, to Stalin's desk in the Kremlin, and he talked, briefly or at length, with Stalin three or four times a week.

Spanish politicians often spoke of him to me as the most powerful man in Spain. That sort of phrase is always meaningless. But it was true that he did play a major role in determining the course of Russian policy in Spain. It was perhaps significant that his favourite literary character was Don Quixote, and when things were relatively quiet he used to invite me to drive out with him to the plateau of La Mancha 'where', he said, 'we can discuss the business of tilting at windmills in an appropriate environment'. We would do that, and later go back to the Palace Hotel and the hot line, and sometimes I could hear Stalin's voice asking questions from the other end.

Throughout the 1930s two tendencies, two policies, two factions, had contended for the direction of Soviet foreign policy. First there were the isolationists. They translated the notion of socialism in one country, forced upon the Bolsheviks by the failure of the revolutionary movements of the West after 1917, into the axiom that the Soviet Union must in no circumstances become engaged in the affairs of the capitalist states, and must refuse any sort of alliance with one capitalist state, of whatever political complexion, against another. Opposed to the isolationists were those who, after Hitler came to power in Germany, believed that the Soviet Union could not afford to isolate itself in this way. If it did so, the result would be a German attack which the West would connive at, or positively encourage. It was therefore essential to take part in what was called collective security; or, in Hitler's language, the encirclement of Germany. But the essential sections of that envisaged arc around Germany were Moscow, Prague and Paris. Spain was peripheral, and nobody in Moscow, of either faction, had bothered to know much more about it than any educated Marxist could dope out from the newspapers. It was known, naturally, as a result of information received from Berlin, that the Spanish Right had for a long time been negotiating with the Nazi government concerning credits, military know-how and smuggled arms. But within days of the outbreak of the rebellion, it became abruptly clear that neither the German nor the Italian government regarded the conflict as peripheral. They obviously rated the importance of Spain much higher than had the Muscovites. Koltzov admitted – and indeed it was evident enough – that thereupon there was considerable flap, hugger-mugger and contention in Moscow, concluding with the defeat of the still meticulously cautious isolationists, and a crash programme for getting, first, military technicians to Spain to assess the situation, and then planes, tanks and other weaponry.

(I happened to be present when the first of those technicians got to the front and were shown round by General Mangada, a Cuban who, as someone said, looked like a cross between Gandhi and his goat, and was one of the few regular generals to remain loyal. The young Russians – described for diplomatic reasons as 'Mexicans' – asked to meet the general's staff. 'No staff', said Mangada. 'In war, staff means betrayal.' They asked if they could take a look at his maps. 'No maps,' said Mangada. 'In war,' he gently stroked his chest, 'the heart must be the map.' The technicians' report caused, as Koltzov told me, much bewilderment in Moscow, and was a useful preview of difficulties to come.)

Though, with the Russian intervention finally under way, there was temporarily something like an equalization of the balance of armaments on both sides, for obvious geographical reasons there was no Russian manpower to counter-balance the Italian divisions engaged on the fascist side. Since the Italians commanded the Mediterranean, the geographical factor very seriously affected the supply of Russian arms too. Looking out to sea from the docks at Valencia, Koltzov once remarked sadly, 'There are enough of our tanks on the bottom of that damned Italian lake to have thrown the Japanese out of Manchuria.'

Despite that, those in Moscow who believed in the practical possibility of collective security for many months believed, first, that victory over fascism in Spain was at least within reach and, secondly, that the defeat of Franco would force, in one way or another, a change in the defeatist or openly pro-fascist attitude of the British Conservative leadership, and hence of the French government. And, their information on the subject being excellent, they knew that such a result would mightily strengthen those elements in the German General Staff which were alarmed by the risks involved for Germany in any general war, and prepared, given enough factual ammunition, to overthrow Hitler rather than run those risks.

But even the enthusiasts for collective security had to admit the possibility that the British Establishment, with the more or less overt support of important Labour and trade union leaders, would regard the victory of the Republicans with Russian support, and with the hugely increased mass adherence to the communists in Spain, notably in the Republican army, as the worst of all possible evils, and that they would, if that outcome looked even probable, exert their diplomatic influence both in Berlin and in Paris to embolden Hitler to use the Russian intervention in Spain as a *casus belli*, an occasion for an immediate attack upon the Soviet Union. And this was what the isolationists had always argued would be the result of the 'outgoing' policy of engagement in an illusory collective security.

It has been repeatedly said that both Berlin and Moscow looked upon Spain as essentially a military testing ground. It was that. But it was also, more importantly, a diplomatic testing ground: testing, specifically, the strength of conflicting tendencies in Britain. It was, for example, regarded as of especial significance that, as the Nazi involvement in Spain increased, Winston Churchill and his faction among the Conservatives courageously reversed the anti-Republican position they had taken up at the beginning of the Civil War.

In the event, these hopeful calculations were proved mistaken. British policy moved further and further towards that appeasement of Hitler which culminated at Munich. Yet, by the end of 1938, although – partly on account of the geographical impediments mentioned – the prospect of absolute victory in Spain was dim, Spanish leaders on both sides, recognizing a military stalemate, were secretly discussing a negotiated peace. But at that juncture, and with that threat of peace looming, the most intransigent of Franco's advisers succeeded in making a new deal with Hitler. They finally mortgaged to the Germans what the Germans had sought all along: control, present and future, of the rich mineral resources of Spain. In return they received a sudden, huge and – in the circumstances of the stalemate – decisive new volume of German military aid.

Professor Hugh Thomas, in his book *The Spanish Civil War*, described this as being among the most important acts of foreign intervention in the war. As he wrote, 'It enabled Franco to mount a new offensive almost immediately . . . Had it not been for this aid (itself the consequence of the German realisation that after Munich nothing they did in the Spanish war would cause Britain or France to go to war over any of its implications), a compromise peace . . . might have been inevitable.'

Inevitable too, with Munich and the defeat in Spain, was the victory of the isolationists in Moscow. Koltzov himself saw with clarity the consequences for Russian policy and for himself. In one of the last conversations I had with him, he previewed in some detail his own fate.

'But,' I said, 'the worst you can be accused of is only that your advice was mistaken.'

'Only?' he said. 'Only? With all that's been at stake, to give mistaken advice can be criminal.'

It was so regarded. In Moscow some months later he was arrested and shot. And with their barbaric slogan 'Viva la Muerte!' the Spanish allies of Marshal Goering occupied the territory of Cervantes.

Brian Crozier

It is impossible for a man of my generation, or older, to be entirely objective about the Spanish Civil War. Hindsight does enable one, however, to impose a new subjectivity on the earlier view – or at any rate to test the judgements formed in the 1930s and 1940s in the light of facts that have emerged since then, and indeed of the history of the intervening years. I have tried to do this, and this has led me to a drastic revision of the views I held in 1939, when the fighting had lately stopped in Spain, and I was twenty-one.

I spent the 1930s in England, and I am not alone in that two dominant realities conditioned my earliest political thinking: the great depression (which, as it happens, hit our family rather badly), and the rise of fascism (and especially of Hitlerism). When the Civil War broke out in 1936, I uncritically accepted the left-wing (and liberal) view, which in its simplest terms was that a parliamentary democracy (good) was being attacked by a fascist-military conspiracy (bad). I joined the Left Book Club and was deeply influenced by Arthur Koestler's account of Franquist atrocities in *A Spanish Testament.*

I regarded Franco's victory as the triumph of our enemies (made possible by Italian and German intervention), and the defeat of our friends (inadequately helped by the Russians and the volunteers of the International Brigades, and betrayed by the non-intervention policy of the democracies).

During the thirty-six or thirty-seven years that have elapsed since the Civil War ended, I have earned my living almost entirely by reporting, commenting on or interpreting international affairs, and have inevitably learned a great deal that I didn't know in 1936–9. During that time, indeed, many new facts about that period have come to light and many new sources have become available. The following seems to me relevant in that these items alone (not counting many others) make it impossible for me to cling to the views of 1939.

The captured German Foreign Ministry archives

The great value of these documents lies in the fact that they were, of course, not intended for publication, and would not, if Germany had not been utterly defeated, have come to light for many years. On study, they show that Franco did not accept Hitler as an ally unconditionally; that he gave as little as he could get away with; and that he stood up, with infuriating obstinacy, to Hitler's threats and blandishments. They show, in particular, that the Fuehrer had precise plans to take Gibraltar, if necessary by invading Spain, but was dissuaded from doing so by a variety of things: the Caudillo's manoeuvrings, the probability that the Spanish armed forces would desperately resist an invasion, and Hitler's mounting problems on the Eastern front.

It was the perusal of the captured German documents that first caused me to doubt the accepted version of the destruction of Guernica, dramatized by Picasso's famous painting. The contemporary Nazi dispatches register surprise and indignation at reports that German aircraft were responsible for the damage. Since they were secret, there was no need for hypocritical reticence. This evidence is supplemented by Nationalist field dispatches (again, not intended for publication), recording that Franco's forces had found the town destroyed by fire, apparently caused by the retreating Republicans.

The view I first expressed in my *Franco* that the Nazis (for all the major atrocities rightly attributed to them) were unlikely to have been responsible for the destruction of Guernica has since been confirmed – unchallengeably, in my opinion – by the expert evidence of an airman who was on the spot a few days after the event, and by the evidence of my own eyes. The point is that it would have been impossible, in the state of aerial bombing technology in 1937 (or indeed at any time until about 1973), for bombers to destroy exactly three-quarters of a small town, leaving the Tree of Guernica and the official buildings untouched.

The controversy, however, goes on, and I have long got used to being accused of ideological bias in the matter, whereas my only concern is with the truth.

The international communist movement

Little was generally known in the late 1930s of the character of the Soviet regime, or of the machinations of the Comintern. Since the war, a mass of information has come to light through the revelations and memoirs of Soviet defectors and through the confessions of non-Russian communists or agents of the Comintern. Arthur Koestler, for example, disclosed in *The Invisible Writing* that he himself had been acting for the Comintern at a time when the world (including myself) thought he was a *bona fide* correspondent of the *News Chronicle* (on which I later served for several years). For that matter, two other *News Chronicle* correspondents in Spain at that time, William Forrest and John Langdon-Davies, were also communists at that time.

In *The Thirties: A Dream Revolved* (1960), Julian Symons provides a graphic description of Koestler's Comintern boss, Willy Muenzenberg, criticizing Koestler and another Comintern writer, Otto Katz, for being too weak and objective: 'Hit them! Hit them hard! Tell the world how they run over their prisoners with tanks, how they pour petrol over them and burn them alive. Make the world gasp with horror . . .'

The dreadful fact is that the reporting of the war in the Western press was overwhelmingly pro-Republican and indelibly coloured by Comintern fabrications. We knew little in those days about the Soviet and communist techniques of disinformation; we know much more now.

From a patient collation of documents and conversations, Burnett Bolloten reconstructed, in *The Grand Camouflage* (1961), the international communist conspiracy to take over the Spanish Republican government from within, and the extraordinary success with which it was hidden from the world by propaganda, disinformation and selective reporting. Much further light on the conspiracy is shed by the memoirs of various communists or ex-communists, including Jesús Hernández Tomás, General Krivitsky and Luigi Longo.

If space permitted, this list of valid reasons for revising my opinions could be greatly extended. It could profitably, for instance, be extended to test the conventional stereotypes of the Spanish Republic and the Franquist state, although to do so would impinge on territory covered by other contributors to this volume. But I have said enough, perhaps, to explain why I found a need for a fundamental reassessment when writing my biography of General Franco, and to prepare the reader for the reflections that follow.

* * *

The international significance of the Spanish Civil War seems to me to lie in three aspects of it, each of which deserves separate treatment: Franco's motives for turning to the Axis powers for help; the motives of the Axis powers in responding to Franco's appeal, and of the Soviet Union in helping the Republic; and the consequences, for Europe and the world, of the Nationalist victory.

Why Franco turned to the Axis

From the start, Franco's role in the Civil War was predominant, but it is worth remembering that he played no part in the initial conspiracy. Indeed the conspirators – especially General Emilio Mola and General José Sanjurjo, at that time in exile in Portugal – were about to act without him, and he decided to join the military rebellion at the last moment. At that time, Francisco Franco, the youngest general in the Spanish army, was himself in semi-exile in the Canary Islands. He held the key to success in the military uprising in that he controlled the Army in Africa, a small but formidable force whose professionalism owed much to Franco's efficient discipline. Having made his way from the Canaries to Morocco, in a British civil plane chartered by the Nationalists, he had the problem of conveying the Army of Africa across the Straits of Gibraltar. It was a daunting one. The bulk of the Spanish fleet was in Republican hands, the crews having turned on their Nationalist officers and murdered them. Any attempted crossing by sea seemed bound to be frustrated by the fleet which, led by the battleship *Jaime I*, was steaming towards the international port of Tangier.

If the fleet had been in Nationalist hands, it is likely that Franco would not have felt the need to turn to the Axis powers. But he had no choice. That he did so was, in the eyes of the world, his 'original sin'. He turned first to Mussolini, who rebuffed his emissary. A second emissary, sent by Mola on 25 July – a week after the uprising began – persuaded *Il Duce* to change his mind. Five days later, Mussolini sent twelve three-engined Italian Savoia-Marchetti 81s to Morocco, of which only nine actually arrived. Meanwhile, two Nazis, at that time living in Morocco, went to see Hitler at Bayreuth, where he was attending a Wagner festival, to put Franco's case for German support.

On the advice of Admiral Canaris, head of German military intelligence – who thought highly of General Franco – he decided to back the Spanish general. Hitler's first planes started arriving. The first group consisted of twenty Junkers 52 maximum-capacity transports and six Heinkel 51 fighters. They immediately started ferrying Nationalist troops across to the mainland. Together, the German and Italian aircraft transported up to 500 men and fifteen tons of material a day across the Straits. Within a few weeks, some 15,000 men were ready for action against the Republic.

Franco then broke the Republican naval blockade – partly by an ultimatum to Tangier to get rid of the fleet (which was accepted), and partly by successfully convoying 3,000 troops from Ceuta to Spain and putting a Republican destroyer to flight although clearly outgunned.

On the Republican side, the government naturally turned to its northern democratic neighbour, the French Republic. Initially, the response of the Popular Front government in Paris was favourable, and thirty-eight French war planes were sent to the Spanish Republicans by 9 August. For a variety of reasons, however, which included the fear of a generalized European war and reluctance to part company with Britain in an appeasing mood, the French soon changed their minds. On the 15th, the French government announced a policy of non-intervention to which Britain and other governments – including those of Germany, Italy and the Soviet Union – soon adhered.

The French nevertheless sent fifty-six more war planes to the Spanish Republic and allowed a small private group of airmen, led by the writer André Malraux, to accompany them. As for Germany, Italy and the Soviet Union, they simply and blatantly disregarded the non-intervention agreement. A small number of Red Air Force planes, together with their pilots, appear to have arrived in eastern Spain from Russia at the beginning of August. On 26 July, the Comintern met in

Prague and decided to raise an international communist volunteer force to help the Republicans. This was the start of the famous International Brigades. At that time, however, Stalin had not committed himself to military aid on a significant scale. Like Hitler and Mussolini, he was watching and waiting.

Why the foreign powers intervened

Essentially, the Spanish Civil War was an indigenous Spanish conflict, although it soon turned into an international ideological battleground. From the start, Mussolini had opposed the Republic, in which he saw a potential for left-wing militancy that might in time threaten his fascist empire. A number of anti-fascist Italians had found refuge in Republican Spain. In turn, Mussolini had given training facilities for small groups of Carlist volunteers on Italian soil. The disastrous efforts of the Spanish Right to overthrow the Republic before the Nationalist uprising, however, had made *Il Duce* sceptical of success from that quarter. But once Mussolini had committed himself, he intervened on the grand scale. Some 50,000 Italian infantrymen went to Spain, together with light tanks and field artillery, fighter planes and bombers. In sum, this was a major commitment of Italian military resources. Although the Italian expeditionary force was heavily defeated at Guadalajara in March 1937, which caused a considerable loss of prestige, Mussolini continued to consider the involvement as a necessary investment; and on the Nationalist side, the Italians were a valuable accretion of manpower.

Hitler was certainly much less emotionally involved in the Spanish war than Mussolini. Having helped Franco at the outset, he cautiously waited to see whether the Nationalists would justify his giving further assistance. He soon decided that they did. His motives were complex. Even in 1936, his hold on the German middle and upper classes was by no means complete. German intervention in Spain was a useful rallying cry to the cause of militant anti-Bolshevism. It contributed to making Germany feared and respected in Europe. And, not least, it provided ideal battle conditions in which to test German weapons and military techniques. Finally, the policy of intervention was a further way of forging the German-Italian Axis – which was formally established in October 1936.

Qualitatively, the German military contribution to Franco's forces was far superior to the Italian. The Condor division was a major contribution to Franco's victory. Germany's heavy artillery and highly trained personnel, heavy bombers and first-class pilots, and anti-aircraft guns with their crews, were the best available on either side in the Spanish war. Moreover, German engineers made an important contribution to the Nationalist effort by building field fortifications, while much of the Nationalist mine-laying operations was supervised by the Germans.

Ideologically, Stalin's intervention was the converse of Hitler's and Mussolini's. The Soviet Union was the only one of the European powers to have intervened politically in Spain before the outbreak of the war. The attempted left-wing revolution of October 1934 (which General Franco had crushed on the orders of the Republican government) was a field day for Comintern subversion. In Spain as in France, the advent of Popular Front policies was encouraged by Comintern agents, who fully exploited the opportunities they offered.

Stalin's violation of the Non-Intervention Agreement was no less blatant and cynical than that of the Axis dictators. Within three days of signing the agreement on 23 August 1936, the Russians appointed Alexander Orlov, a high-ranking N.K.V.D. officer, to advise the Republican government in Spain on intelligence, counter-intelligence and guerilla warfare. It is improbable that Stalin initially proposed to foster a communist regime in Spain. From the revelations of Orlov after his defection, and of another leading defector, Walter Krivitsky, what Stalin aimed at was establishing a predominant position of influence within the Republican government. The Spanish Communist Party would be represented in the government, but only by one or two ministers, so as to reassure the Western democracies. A further purpose of intervention in Stalin's eyes was probably to divert the attention of Western intellectuals from the great purges being carried out in the U.S.S.R. itself. For could his regime seriously be accused of practising terror on a vast scale at a time when the Soviet Communist Party was so clearly involved in fighting for freedom and democracy in Spain?

It is worth remembering, incidentally, that Stalin's aid to the Spanish Republic was not provided gratis: payment was in fact made by the transfer of most of the Bank of Spain's gold reserve to Russia.

When the Civil War actually began, events soon took a turn which Stalin may not have foreseen, with a sweeping anarchist revolution, in which records were destroyed, prisons were emptied, property was seized, church buildings were burned and the clergy were tortured and killed. In the second phase, however, the communists carried out a carefully planned takeover of the Republican state under the close supervision of Comintern officers who, for Stalin's purposes, 'used' such public figures as Largo Caballero and Premier Negrín (who shipped the Republic's gold to Russia). The takeover would doubtless have been more complete had it not been for Stalin's reluctance to let it be apparent to the world that the Spanish Communist Party was in control of the Republican government. If the Republican forces had won, Spain would probably not have been a parliamentary democracy but a communist-controlled 'people's democracy'.

On the military side, at one stage Soviet aid to the Republic exceeded Axis aid to the Nationalists. But this situation did not last. Apart from material assistance, Comintern agents closely supervised and organized the recruiting of foreign volunteers for the International Brigades. These included some adventurers and riff-raff, a high proportion of idealists and a strong controlling cadre of highly trained communists. The best evidence is that they totalled about 35,000. Some estimates range higher – to 50,000 or 60,000. But even if the higher figures are accepted, foreigners fighting on the Republican side would have been outnumbered about two to one by those helping the Nationalists. There were very few Russian nationals in Spain – and those were mostly observers, advisers and technicians. The Republican air force, however, was dominated by the Russians. For them as well as for the Germans and Italians, Spain was a useful proving ground. Altogether about 1,000 Soviet pilots gained battle experience during the Spanish war.

By mid-1937, the Spanish communists had achieved a dominant political and military position in the Republican areas. At this point, Stalin began to reduce his interventionist effort.

The Germans went on in full strength until the spring of 1938, when Hitler had carried through his *Anschluss* with Austria, and was getting ready to occupy Czechoslovakia. The Italians went on wholeheartedly to the end.

The consequences of Franco's victory

In the polarized situation of 1936–9, it became fashionable on the

Nationalist side to lump all Republicans together as 'Reds' and communists, and on the Republican side to label all Franco's supporters 'fascists'. These labels were misleading, but they stuck. In fact, Franco led a coalition of political forces right of centre, which probably only he could have united under one banner: the monarchists (both Carlists and Alfonsists), big business and the landed gentry, the Church (except in the Basque provinces), traditionalist army officers, and the 'fascist' Falange. Franco appeared to confirm the fascist label, when he turned to the Falange in search of a viable ideology: only the Falange had one. But the ruling political group he created was a very diluted form of 'fascism'. One of its purposes was undoubtedly to persuade his German and Italian supporters that he was truly on their side.

When the Second World War broke out in 1939, Hitler and Mussolini assumed – as did the democracies – that Spain would join the war on the side of the Axis. But Franco had no such intention. He had saluted the Nazi and Italian contingents in his victory parade, but lost no time thereafter in getting rid of them. Proclaiming Spain's neutrality or non-belligerency (the formula varied to meet the fluctuations of fortune in the Second World War), Franco – as I have noted – resisted all Hitler's threats and blandishments. Gibraltar stayed in British hands, the Allied campaign in north Africa was safeguarded, and Rommel was defeated. In the House of Commons on 25 May 1944, Winston Churchill praised Franco Spain's contribution to the Allied success in the Mediterranean. At the Nuremberg Tribunal after the war, General Alfred Jodl, Chief of the Operations Staff of the German High Command, declared that it was 'General Franco's repeated refusal to allow German forces to pass through Spain to take Gibraltar' that had been one of the major causes of Germany's defeat.

Had Franco been defeated in the Spanish war, and had a near-communist Spain emerged, Hitler would probably have invaded the country after defeating France, and have captured Gibraltar. There would have been no Franco to tangle him in double-talk. The Allied campaigns in north Africa would almost certainly have become impossible, and the United States might well have stayed out of the European war.

All this of course is hypothetical, but there can be no doubt of the paradoxical consequence of Franco's victory: against all expectations, it contributed to the defeat of Hitler.

3—TDD * *

Despite these facts, the fascist label did stick, and Spain was ostracized for many years after the defeat of the Axis powers, deprived of Marshall Aid for postwar reconstruction, and kept out of NATO. The ostracism continued even after Franco – the least ideological of twentieth-century dictators – had broken the original Falangist followers of José Antonio Primo de Rivera and demoralized them in the course of perpetuating his own power by playing off one faction against another within Spain. Thus the Caudillo continued to pay the price of his 'original sin'.

Peter Kemp

When I left London for Spain on a wet and windy morning in early November 1936 I certainly did not expect to be at war for nearly ten years; I intended to be away for about six months. I went to join the Nationalist army for a variety of motives, the first of which was simply a craving for adventure, not unusual at the age of twenty-one. I had come down from Cambridge the previous June with a degree in classics and law, and was continuing my studies for the Bar when the Civil War broke out on 18 July. At public school and university, as well as at home, my life had been easy and secure; I had seen very little of the world outside Britain. Now was my chance, before I settled into some dull job, to test myself in hardship and hazard and to get to know a new country and people – even to learn a new language, for I spoke no word of Spanish.

My second motive was rather more idealistic. I had been active in politics at Cambridge, where my traditionalist, Tory opinions caused me to view both communism and fascism with equal loathing. But of the two I believed communism presented the greater danger to Europe. In 1936 the threat from Germany and Italy was not so clear, at least to me, as it became later, and at the beginning of the Civil War the Nationalists were not receiving very obvious or extensive help from either country. In France, however, communists were already active in the *Front Populaire* government, and a careful study of the early uncensored newspaper reports from Madrid and Barcelona convinced me that the communist party was, or soon would be, in control of the Spanish Republic. Within weeks of the outbreak of fighting the Western

Department of the Comitern was busy recruiting, equipping and training the International Brigades, by far the best troops in the Republican army; their senior officers and political commissars were veteran communists.

I was also deeply shocked by accounts in those same newspaper dispatches of the widespread and indiscriminate massacres in Republican territory of 'enemies of the people' – the clergy and others whose position or means rendered them objects of suspicion or mere envy. I was not a Roman Catholic, but it seemed to me that Christian values, law and order, and the security of my own country would alike be threatened by a Republican victory. I also felt, naively perhaps but strongly, that if I had been prepared to proclaim my opinions in the safety of the Cambridge Union, I should also be ready to defend them on the battlefield. I am only too well aware that many of my contemporaries went to fight, for very similar reasons, on the opposite side.

The Nationalists had no recruiting machinery in England, but a chance meeting with their agent in London brought me an introduction to some officers on the General Staff at Nationalist headquarters in Burgos. They suggested I should join one of the two militia formations – either the Falange (fascists) or the Carlists. I rejected the Falange without hesitation, but everything I knew about the Carlists appealed to me. Originating in the bitter dynastic struggles of the nineteenth century, the Carlists, or *Requetés*, combined a deeply devout Catholicism with a passionate devotion to their country and its ancient traditions; their programme was monarchy, regional autonomy and paternal rule, expressed in their motto, *Dios, Fueros, Patria y Rey*, 'God, our liberties, country, and King'. Their heartland was in the Basque provinces of Navarre and Alava, although they had a strong following in the other two Basque provinces, which were in Republican hands. This was a civil war not only between Spaniards but also between Basques.

It is easy today to ridicule the Carlist faith as a romantic anachronism, but it inspired its followers to a self-sacrificing heroism in battle that won them universal praise throughout Spain – a country where courage is almost taken for granted. Within two weeks of the outbreak of the war there was scarcely a young man left in Navarre. They formed the backbone of General Mola's armies in the north. But many of them only learned to load their rifles on the way to the front, and their reckless bravery, combined with their lack of training and discipline and their crazy insistence on wearing their distinctive scarlet berets in action, caused them terrible casualties.

By this time the war in the north was at a standstill; the fighting was concentrated around Madrid, where the unexpected arrival of the International Brigades had stopped the Nationalist advance in the outskirts of the city. And so I hurried south to Toledo, carrying letters from my friends on the General Staff to the Carlist commanders there; a few days later I enrolled as a trooper in a squadron of *Requeté* cavalry quartered in a village halfway between Toledo and Talavera.

The squadron commander was the only English speaker; my fellow tropers were Andalusians whose guttural dialect was incomprehensible to me, even with the help of my Hugo's Spanish Grammar. But officers and men alike made me welcome, and I soon picked up enough to take part in the squadron's duties. These were chiefly to guard the Toledo-Talavera road and patrol the olive groves beside the Tagus, and to give warning of any attempt to cross over by the enemy beyond the river. But this was a quiet sector, and the nearest I came to battle was a mounted charge against a herd of goats which our scouts had mistaken in the distance for Republican *milicianos*.

It was obvious that cavalry would be useless in the street fighting and trench warfare around Madrid, and so in mid-December I managed to transfer to an infantry battalion operating in the suburb of Carabanchel. It was a sharp and uncomfortable contrast to my quiet life beside the Tagus. I was attached to a platoon holding a small group of houses which formed a salient surrounded on three sides by buildings, only a few yards away, occupied by the Republicans. Day and night hand-grenades and mortar bombs rained down on us and enemy fire came from all directions; we dared not raise our voices above a whisper. Only at night could we receive supplies from the rear, or send back our wounded. Although it had no tactical importance, and cost us heavy casualties, our troops continued to hold this salient until, soon after my platoon was relieved, the Republicans blew up the position with a mine. This expensive obstinacy in holding on to useless positions, towns or territory for reasons of prestige was a feature of the Civil War.

After a hurried visit to England following the sudden death of my father, I found myself attached in February 1937 to a battalion of

Requetés holding a line of low hills overlooking the valleys of the Manzanares and Jarama, about eight miles south of Madrid. The bloody battle of the Jarama, which lasted most of February, was an unsuccessful attempt by the Nationalists to cut the Madrid-Valencia road, the last remaining direct link between the capital and the Republican bases on the Mediterranean. The role of my battalion, under a gallant but choleric major who had survived the siege of the Alcázar, was the important one of protecting the left flank of the Nationalist advance. I was therefore surprised to see how badly laid out our trenches were: they ran in a continuous line along the hill crests, with no traverses, and were much too shallow. Spanish troops, *Requetés* particularly but also the crack Foreign Legion, seemed to think it undignified to dig trenches deep enough to give proper protection from shell fire.

When, therefore, the Republicans attacked us under cover of an artillery bombardment our casualties were much higher than they need have been, and we only just held on to the position after two days of hard fighting. It was partly the courage of the *Requetés* that saved us, partly the arrival at a critical moment of a squadron of our tanks, but chiefly the inept and suicidal tactics of the enemy. They put in a frontal assault in broad daylight across a plain dominated by our positions and almost devoid of cover. Their artillery preparation, though unpleasant enough for us, was quite inadequate for such a task, and their losses were appalling. They were Spanish troops and I greatly admired their bravery, but I wondered what kind of military cretin had ordered such an attack. I believe the main reason why the Republicans lost the war – apart from their initial failure to hold command of the sea – was their ignorance of tactics, planning, and logistics and – except in the International Brigades – the inferior quality of their officers.

In this action I saw the *Requeté* spirit in its most romantic – and wholly unprofessional – aspect. My companions exposed themselves quite recklessly to enemy fire, leaning right over the parapet in their eagerness to get a better shot. Frequently one of them would slump forward, riddled with bullets, and roll some way down the forward slope; whereupon our company chaplain* would run down after him, the purple tassel of his scarlet beret streaming in the wind, and kneel

* The Carlist formations had a chaplain to each company, not one to a battalion like the rest of the army.

over him administering the last rites while bullets spattered the earth all round him. Our company commander walked calmly up and down the parados behind the trenches, clearly silhouetted against the skyline, encouraging us and controlling our fire, until his shoulder was shattered by a machine-gun burst.

Our chaplain, Father Vicente, was a throwback to a darker Crusading age. When the enemy was on the run he darted hither and thither among us, pointing out targets among the fleeing Republicans and exhorting us not to let any get away. I met him again a few months later in the final attack on the heights overlooking Bilbao – a day of carnage that cost the battalion some sixty per cent in casualties. He personally led the assault in his scarlet and purple beret and mounted on a white horse. Few around him survived, but he escaped with a bullet in the arm; and the following day, a Sunday, he preached an impassioned sermon to the victorious troops with his arm in a sling, repeating at frequent intervals the refrain: 'Against God it is impossible to fight!'

After the capture of Bilbao in June 1937 there was little more fighting on that northern front, and I saw none of it. I did, however, learn something about the famous Guernica controversy through my friendship with a British and a French journalist who entered the town with the first Nationalist troops to occupy it, and who closely examined the damage and questioned many of the inhabitants. This was the communists' most successful single propaganda *coup* of the war, and it created a myth which, fostered by the skill of Agitprop and immortalized by the genius of Picasso, has passed into history. According to this myth Guernica was razed by German Stukas as an experiment in dive bombing. The truth is that the town, an important communications centre and a divisional H.Q., was bombed by the Nationalist air force – not the German – who hit the railway station and an arms factory; later it was dynamited and set on fire by the retreating *milicianos* – mostly squads of Asturian miners.*

By the autumn of 1937 the character of the Civil War had changed from an amateur, if not exactly light-hearted, exercise into a grim contest between professionals. Moreover, there was a growing likelihood of a world war to follow. For both these reasons I felt I had better

* See also Brian Crozier's *Franco*, pp. 246–7 (Eyre and Spottiswoode, 1967). The frontier town of Irun was similarly destroyed, as was widely reported at the time.

try to turn myself into a serious soldier. After some considerable difficulty and delay I arranged a transfer in my existing rank of ensign to the *Tercio* or Spanish Foreign Legion, and at the end of October was posted to the 14th Bandera (Battalion).

Formed in 1920 by Generals Millán Astray and Franco for service in the Moroccan war, this élite corps was by far the most efficient, best trained and best equipped force in the Nationalist army. Its officers and men, bound together in a tradition of courage, self-sacrifice and endurance, were deployed, like the International Brigades on the other side, as 'shock troops' in situations of the most critical importance or the greatest danger. All were volunteers. Ninety per cent of the men and almost all the officers were Spaniards; the remainder were mostly Portuguese. Off duty the legionary enjoyed considerable freedom, but in the field discipline was severe and punishments arbitrary and often savage.

On joining my bandera I was at first given a platoon of four machine-guns – 1916 Maxims captured from the Republicans; I had no idea how they worked, but luckily my sergeants had. Neither my company nor bandera commanders were at all pleased to be saddled with so inexperienced an officer – and an Englishman at that. In consequence I was chased remorselessly, and no mistake or omission was overlooked or left unreprimanded; I was told sharply to improve my Spanish. At the end of three months I had learned fluent if not drawing room Spanish and become as nearly efficient an officer as my indolent and unpractical nature would allow. After I had fought a couple of actions with the bandera I was accepted; but I was never allowed to forget, even had I wished to, how privileged I was as a foreigner to hold a commission in the Legion.

The Battle of Teruel, which lasted from mid-December 1937 to the end of February 1938, gave me an unwelcome taste of war in sub-zero temperatures. The fighting caused both sides fearful losses, and so also did the cold; the 1st Navarre Division, for example, had 3,500 casualties from frostbite between 31 December and 5 January – all this for a town of no conceivable military value. My bandera operated during February in the mountains north of Teruel. All day we marched and fought under a hot sun. At night we lay down to sleep in the snow, often without blankets or even greatcoats, which we had had to leave behind, and without fires, which would have betrayed our position to the enemy. Daylight would usually reveal the stiff corpses of two or three legionaries who had died of cold in the night.

In the middle of February we launched an attack against Americans and Canadians of the 15th International Brigade entrenched on a ridge in the sierra, but we made no headway against intensive machine-gun fire supported by artillery and mortars. In the two-day battle we suffered over 100 killed and badly wounded, including my company commander; three out of my four Maxims were destroyed. We dug in to lick our wounds in the snow-bound pine woods.

On 9 March began the great Nationalist offensive that in less than six weeks carried their armies from Saragossa to the Mediterranean. It was conducted on *blitzkrieg* lines, and the 14th and 16th Banderas formed the spearhead of the initial advance. I had transferred, at my own request, to a rifle company commanded by a very gallant and amiable captain with no anti-British prejudices. A powerful air and artillery bombardment shattered the Republican defences, and for six days we pressed forward, sometimes covering twenty miles a day on foot, including frequent deployments to storm hastily improvised Republican positions. But on the seventh day a heavy counter-attack by the 14th International Brigade, among others, halted us in our tracks, and in the ensuing twenty-four hours both banderas were lucky to escape annihilation. My company suffered seventy-five per cent casualties, and I myself was wounded three times, although not seriously apart from grenade splinters in my arm. At one point in the battle it seemed to me quite inevitable that I should be killed; curiously in that moment I felt it was worthwhile. Our adversaries, I learned afterwards, were British.

When I rejoined the bandera after three months in hospital we were holding a bridgehead across the River Segre, on the borders of Aragon and Catalonia – an uncomfortable position under constant bombardment from artillery and mortars. On 23 July a mortar bomb burst beside me, shattering my jaw and severely damaging both hands. Left at first for dead, I was eventually taken to a forward hospital where a brilliant surgeon operated – without anaesthetic – and saved my life. By the time I was fit for active duty, in March 1939, the war was over.

In November 1938 I was given leave to convalesce in England, where I discovered that for all their victories on the battlefield the

Nationalists had lost the war of propaganda. Their treatment of journalists had always been unenlightened, to say the least, whereas the Republican press campaign, ably directed by the Comintern – as Arthur Koestler has shown – was brilliant, unscrupulous, and effective. I learned to my surprise that the Nationalist armies and air force were manned almost exclusively by German and Italian mercenaries, and that the cause for which I had risked and nearly lost my life was fascism. There was hardly any mention of the vital Russian help to the Republicans.

There were in fact two divisions of Italians and two 'mixed' divisions of Italians and Spaniards with the Nationalists; the Germans provided instructors and technicians, notably communications specialists, but no fighting troops. At the start of the war both sides employed foreign air crews – the Spanish Air Force scarcely existed – until they had trained sufficient Spaniards; and throughout the war both depended on foreign war material. But after the spring of 1937 it is a fact that the Nationalist forces on land, sea and in the air were overwhelmingly Spanish. As for fascism, the Falange were numerically insignificant at the outbreak of the war, and contributed almost nothing to the fighting. My *Requeté* companions regarded them with strong distaste, my fellow legionaries with contempt. When I pointed out these truths few people listened. History, it has been well said, is the propaganda that sticks.

II

Eyewitnesses

Shiela Grant Duff

A VERY BRIEF VISIT

It was February 1937 and I was in Prague when a telegram arrived from Edgar Mowrer of the *Chicago Daily News* asking me to 'undertake an important assignment in Western Europe'. I had worked in Edgar's office in Paris and learned from him, as much as from anyone, that the only decent aim for any foot-free individual at that moment in history was the defeat of fascism. Prague had been his suggestion for the key-post to take up in that struggle but little was as yet happening there, and I looked with envy and admiration at my friends fighting in Spain or running Spanish Aid Committees in London or Paris.

I rang Edgar to ask if this was at last a chance to join them. 'If I could have told you about it on the telephone, I would have rung myself,' he said curtly. 'Either you come or you don't come.'

I went. I took the train leaving Prague that night and was in the Place de l'Opéra next day, climbing the stairs – or more probably taking the lift – to Edgar's office.

'This is no ordinary assignment,' he said. 'If it had been, we would have sent one of our own correspondents. The *Chicago Daily News* doesn't see eye to eye with Franco and we back the Spanish government so Franco hasn't much use for us. That's why we want to send somebody totally unknown and who won't be taken seriously.'

'Too true,' I sighed.

'Actually, you're going for the Spanish government and the *Chicago Daily News* is only the cover. It won't get you out of any scrapes so you had better not get into any. The first thing is for you to meet the Spanish government agent here. He goes under the name of André Simon – a marvellous man, a German Jew with a duelling scar.'

'Fine,' I said. 'Where do I find him?'

'You don't find him at all. Let's get this straight. No monkeying about. It's a dangerous assignment and to be seen talking to André Simon in Paris and followed to Franco's Spain would not be funny. You and I will go out in my car and he will find us. He will sit in the back and tell you what he wants you to do while we drive round Paris.'

This we duly did. André Simon was Otto Katz, a German from Prague, I believe, and a Comintern agent. (It was in Prague that he was eventually executed when Stalin liquidated a number of his friends in the fifties.) I learned all this much later. At the time I thought he was a nice Frenchman.

He told me he wanted me to go to Malaga, which Franco had just taken and into which no Western correspondent had yet been allowed. It was vital for the cause of the Spanish Republic that news should be published of the appalling slaughter which succeeded Franco's entry into every Spanish town. It would also be a strong card to play in the Non-intervention Committee if it could be proved that Franco was fortifying Malaga harbour as a naval base for the Axis in the event of war.

Before I could question him, Simon jumped out of the car and made off. Edgar drove me back to the Hôtel de I'Université where I was staying. 'There is one more thing I wish you to do,' he said. 'Arthur Koestler is in prison in Malaga. Try and get him out or at least go and see him and make a fuss so that he doesn't just disappear. Tomorrow we will make all the arrangements. Let me have a look at your passport.'

In those days, passports were stamped as one crossed every frontier, and I was particularly proud of the number of frontiers I had crossed. Two of them were those of the Soviet Union, which I had entered from Poland and left from Leningrad. 'You'll have to get a new one,' he said. 'The British embassy will issue it when you explain you are going to Franco's Spain.' Surprisingly they did, and on the nail.

'How do I actually reach Malaga?' I asked.

'You fly – no direct planes of course, because it's still in the battle zone. You can go through north Africa and approach it from Gibraltar. The last part may be a bit rough.'

'That's all right,' I said proudly, 'I've brought my skiing clothes.'

'Skiing clothes!' he exclaimed. 'Perfect nonsense. You wear your prettiest dress and stand by the side of the road with a bunch of flowers and an Italian officer will give you a lift.'

'Oh Lord!' I thought, 'worse than death as well as death.' We were all rather prim in those days and I primmer than most. I admit I was also scared, but there was no getting out of it.

'I don't speak a word of Spanish,' I said. 'How am I going to find anything out?'

'We've got a first-class American consul there,' said Edgar. 'He's been through the whole period. He hates Franco. He'll tell you everything you want to know. A really good chap – solidly pro-government.'

I went to bed feeling it was my last night in the world I knew. I couldn't even say goodbye because Edgar had forbidden me to tell anyone I was going. Like Arthur Koestler, I thought, I may just disappear.

Next evening, armed with a new passport, lots of money, a sleeper-berth to Bordeaux and an air ticket to Valencia-Oran-Casablanca-Tangier, I boarded a train and slept. It was still dark at the Bordeaux aerodrome next morning, and the hectic flares and revving engines alarmed me considerably. I had never flown before, and as I climbed into the plane I felt I was entering my tomb. As we soared over the Pyrenees, the rising sun flooded earth and sky with such radiant beauty that I ceased to be afraid. Things are always more frightening before you come to them. Thereafter I was quite brave.

I came to Gibraltar with a useful introduction – to the governor himself. Shortly before this he had sent a naval vessel to the Spanish coast to collect Jessica Mitford and Giles Romilly who had run away together to Spain. I saw no reason why a naval vessel should not equally be used to put me ashore. In the thirties we still believed that His Majesty's officials abroad were not only all-powerful but were there to serve His Majesty's subjects. Why should they care less for my safety than that of two of my more distant cousins?

Before calling on the admiral, I had investigated the frontier at La Linea and they had tried to impound my passport on the understanding that it would be returned when I left Spain. My mission was such that I thought I might not be wanting to stop for a passport on the way out. I realized I could not make this point nor confide the nature of my mission to the charming admiral who received me, so I started the conversation as innocently as possible.

Could he tell me, I asked naively, how I could get to Malaga?

'Ah,' he said, 'that is a difficult one. It has only just been liberated. I must ask one of my advisers.'

He rang the bell importantly and an exceedingly unimportant young man came smartly in.

'Miss Grant Duff,' said the admiral, 'wishes to go to Malaga. Have you any suggestions how she should proceed?'

'She can take a taxi,' said the maddening young man. 'The taxi-driver won't, of course, stay overnight in belligerent country but she would have a few hours there to look round.'

'I want more than a few hours,' I said firmly, 'a few days at least.'

'That is more difficult,' he said, proceeding to treat my problem as if it were a matter of travelling to Orpington during a railway strike. 'If all the taxis in La Linea and Algeciras have not been commandeered, you may find a Spanish taxi-driver who might consent to stay a day or two in Malaga. It will cost you quite a lot.'

I was not in my skiing clothes nor even in that pretty dress with a bunch of flowers but he rightly appraised my incapacity for spending money. I had paid for all my journeys over Europe so far myself. The Spanish government was now paying expenses – there had been no other mention of money, nor was there ever subsequently – but this was the cause of the have-nots against the haves. Not a moment for expensive taxis. Nor easy, really, to bridge the gap between the taxi they suggested and the gun-boat I was hoping to get round to. I was bowed out of the presence with much shaking of hands and wishing me well. I had no one else to turn to except the porter at my hotel. He suggested a boat trip to Algeciras and further enquiries there.

As my little package steamer chugged into the harbour of this war-torn country, a most surprising sight greeted my eyes: a line of hotel porters with the names of the hotels they worked for printed on their hat bands. I chose one reassuringly called BRITANNIA and told him my problem. He took it even more prosaically than the naval young man. 'There is a bus,' he cried triumphantly. 'It leaves in half an hour. I will take you there.'

I boarded the bus. It was at least in keeping with my means if not with my idea of my dangerous and dramatic mission. It sped merrily through the countryside, picking up and deposing large jolly peasant women and their baskets. There were occasional road blocks and searches but no one boarded our bus, which hooted its way past every obstacle. It seemed no time before we were entering Malaga. There was little sign of devastation but also little sign of normal busy life. I had never been in Spain nor in a civil war, so I did not know what to expect. What I saw was slow, uneventful, almost deserted.

I made my way to the hotel whose name had been given me by my hall porter. He was quite firm that this was the only place to go. It was early evening and the light was fading fast. I felt I had no time to lose and enquired immediately for the American consul's residence – no telephone was working. They said it was some distance and as there were no taxis they did not advise me to be out on the streets after dark. I said that I must go immediately, and armed with a street plan I left the hotel.

It was not difficult to find the house but quite impossible to get into it. It was surrounded by a high wall which enclosed the garden; the only door was firmly shut. A passing Spaniard, seeing me hammering on it, made me understand that no one would come, as night had fallen. I made him understand the absolute necessity of my getting inside, so he kindly assisted me over the wall. I crossed the garden and rang the house bell. The door was half-opened by a maid who kept the chain in place while she fetched her mistress.

With Edgar's letter in their hands, the consul and his wife welcomed me in – a bit shocked that I had come through dark streets and scaled their wall but friendly enough. I asked if the streets were really so dangerous for I had seen nothing and encountered very few people.

'Oh well,' said the consul, 'it's a bit better now, but when the Reds ruled this city, there was nightly butchery and it was safe to go nowhere.'

This didn't sound to me very 'solidly pro-government', and I tried asking innocently whether the Franco side was really more law-abiding and well-behaved than the government. The consul looked at me sharply but his wife, quite unabashed, declared: 'Oh! They're all as ghastly as each other. I wouldn't cross a drawing room floor to shake any Spaniard by the hand.'

At that moment the door opened and three young Spaniards entered. It was the consul who crossed the drawing room floor to meet them, shaking them warmly by the hand. They greeted his wife like old and welcome friends and showed polite deference to me. It was clear that they were expected – and not for the first time – to dinner, and we all sat down together to a good Spanish meal. I was hungry. I was also alerted that I had not much to hope for in the way of help or information from the consul.

It transpired that these three young men were all members of Franco's staff and, since my hotel had been commandeered by Franco for his own use, we were all staying under the same roof. They would conduct me, said the consul, through those dangerous streets. The young men seemed amused that I had been given a bedroom in their staff headquarters and laughingly told me that the Reds had melted down all the bedroom keys for arms so I must look out. They were rather charming young men, with Spanish grandee manners which couldn't fail to please – no need of a bunch of flowers with them. One had been at Cambridge and one was Jewish, both of which facts I found reassuring; the third, however, had red hair, which I found particularly sinister on a Spaniard.

I did not gather much useful information from the dinner-time conversation. A great deal of it was about mutual friends; still more about mutual enemies and the appalling atrocities committed against priests and princes, nuns and women. In those days, we innocents of the Left did not believe these stories. It was all wicked propaganda and our hands, and the hands of our friends, were clean. I suppose I betrayed a certain lack of horror and indignation, for when we got back to the hotel they insisted on showing me photographs and became angry at my unwillingness to look at them. But they were drinking heavily and on the whole were bright and gay. On their side it was a flirtation rather than a political encounter. Suddenly one of them looked at his watch.

'Good Heavens!' he said. 'Twenty minutes to midnight. Do you want to come to an execution with us?'

Silence fell and all three looked at me. I felt confronted as I had never felt confronted before with a stark choice whose consequences would stay with me forever. For a young journalist it would be a sensational *coup*; for a spy it would really be seeing what Franco's men were at; for a human being it would be to stand and watch people whom I regarded as friends and allies being put to death in cold blood. I knew I would never be able to live with it. I did not go. Instead, I went to bed and wedged a chair under the handle of my door so no one could enter, key or no key.

I awoke to spring sunshine. I went down to the terrace. They had rolled little orange trees into the garden and the fruit was warming in the sun. There were swallows flying low over the water, and sky and sea were shades of the same deep azure blue. The young men were drinking coffee. Still in military uniform, they now had revolvers in their belts. I thought of Prague with its leaden wintry skies, the snow piled in dirty sodden heaps on the pavements, the ill-clad Czechs shuffling along with their shoulders hunched against the cold. I turned on the laughing young men and said: 'You have a country like this where the sun is warm in February and the skies are blue and there are swallows. How can you have a civil war?'

'Now, now,' said the one from Cambridge, 'you are talking like a Red.'

'If that's how they feel . . .' I started. Double-bluff? Clever? They didn't think so. The sinister one with red hair turned on me.

'Who exactly are you?' I handed him my passport. The effect was electric. 'It is less than a week old,' he exclaimed. 'It was issued in Paris not by the Foreign Office. How did you get here? No journalist has yet been allowed into Malaga. The front is only a few miles up the road. We are off there now. When we get back, I wish to look into your credentials.'

'Your representative in Tangier gave me a press card,' I said.

'It is useless. You must go to Seville and come through the proper channels.'

They rose from their seats, saluted and walked out.

I had no intention of going to Seville nor of being investigated, so I saw I had one day, and one day only, to find out what Mowrer and Simon wanted. I had drawn a blank with the American consul, I would see what the British could do.

I found the consul in his office and explained my predicament vis-à-vis the Franco aides. He confirmed that they were acting within their rights and could certainly have me sent to Seville. I told him about the executions and asked him what was going on. He admitted that Franco's men were rounding up people all the time but there was, he said, the semblance of a trial. He told me where I could attend these courts. I asked him about Koestler and told him my instructions from Mowrer. 'You would be extremely ill-advised in your equivocal position to raise any sort of question about Koestler,' he said. 'It would do him no good and you considerable harm. Forget it.'

I began to feel Mowrer and Simon had made a bad choice when they sent me to Malaga. I could not see how I was going to find out any of the information they wanted and I was obviously going to be of no use to Arthur Koestler.

I left the consul and walked down to the harbour. Several sentries were standing in front of the iron gates which sealed the port. Though dressed in the semblance of military uniform, I guessed that their ages could not have been more than fourteen or fifteen. I presented my press card. The brightest of them pointed out that it gave me no right of entry to places of military importance.

'Ah,' I said, in what I hoped was Spanish, 'this is of naval importance.' I must have said something convincing for he immediately saluted and opened the gate. I wandered through the docks. There was the same atmosphere of things at a standstill. There were crates lying about everywhere, most of them empty, some filled with oranges. There were piles of rotting oranges on the quays, little else. There were few ships in port and none of them bore any resemblance to an armed naval vessel. I wondered if a port could be fortified without it being obvious to the naked eye. I wandered right out to the entrance and saw my first armament – a machine-gun, indeed two, one on each side of the harbour mouth. The posts were not even manned. I could not see that much could be made of this information in the Non-intervention Committee.

In the afternoon I went to the court. The place was unimpressive, more like a small hall where election meetings are held in country districts in England than any law court I'd ever seen. The proceedings had been going on all day; every day since Franco's men had entered the town, men – and a few women, very few – had been brought in and questioned. They looked miserable, as prisoners everywhere look miserable. They spoke in low voices as the cowed always speak. Each had only a few minutes to say his say and was then led out. I understood not one word that was spoken, neither by the accused nor the accusers.

Again I thought guiltily of my mission and how I was failing. I found someone at the back of the hall who spoke and understood a little French. He told me all the prisoners were condemned. All I could do was to make rough calculations as to the numbers. I had failed over the manner of the executions, now I was failing over the excuses given for them.

I went out and wandered round the town, hoping something would present itself to my view which would justify the whole expedition. The devastation of civil war was less than that which I had seen in Belgium as a child, years after the Great War had ended. Could the tragedy of civil war be still deeper in the flesh of these wretched people with whom I could not communicate? Every woman seemed to be draped in black, every man – but men were few – seemed to wear a black arm band. Their hair was black, their eyes were black, their faces grey and pinched. I thought of the sunshine and the swallows on the terrace in the morning. If these people in their black hovels had started the war, I could have understood, but those young men in their smart uniforms, with their clean-shaven faces, their smiling eyes, their gay contempt? I did not want to meet them again. They would be back late, they said, and see me in the morning.

I am better at getting up in the mornings than most people – indeed, the mornings are my special joy and the next morning was no exception. Long before the young men descended to the terrace for their coffee, I was on my way. The bus for La Linea left early and I was on it. Once again we sped gaily down the road, honking our way through every road barrier, alone of all the transport on that road not to be searched, not to be delayed. It was with self-satisfaction that I saw cars pulled up by the side of the road with G.B. number plates. One, indeed, even had a C.D., and its occupants had been decanted on to the verge. The peasant women in my bus waved and laughed and we sailed on. At La Linea I made a roundabout walk from the bus stop to the frontier post – unnecessarily, for no one took any notice of me. On the Spanish side of the frontier a long line of cars was halted and the frontier officials were going slowly through them.

I remembered my experiences as a London school girl when I used often to take devious routes home for which I did not have the fare, being given each morning just what it cost for my bus. In those days if one walked with confidence past the barriers at underground stations no one stopped one. I thought I would try it now, though I estimated my danger to be much greater than it probably was. Those horrible young men, I felt certain, were by now hot on my trail and would take ruthless steps to carry me off to Seville. I had been warned that no correspondent was allowed out of the country immediately after a visit to the fighting zone. My press card, therefore, was now a liability rather than a protection. I was tempted to ask for a lift in one of the stationary G.B. cars, but my experience of hitch-hiking was less than my experience of walking unconcernedly through barriers. I opted for the latter.

I had not anticipated the huge empty no man's land which lies between frontier posts. I passed the Spanish guards easily – they were all occupied with the cars – but as I walked across the empty space to the British lines I expected every moment shouts and running feet. I resisted the temptation to run myself or to look behind me, and as I came up to the British sentries I resisted also the temptation to fling my arms round their necks. Never had I loved my fellow countrymen more dearly.

* * *

The rest was uneventful. Forgetting Mowrer's conviction that no one would take me seriously, I was still frightened in the train crossing Spanish Morocco. It would have seemed to me in no way preposterous had the red-haired Spaniard been waiting on the frontier to arrest me.

In Paris I was easily reduced to size. Mowrer and Simon made no bones about their contemptuous disappointment. The very insignificance of the bill I put in for my expenses seemed to confirm the insignificance of the information I brought back. Mowrer was rightfully indignant about his American consul and equally contemptuous about my refusal to go to the execution. For him, Germany had put the clock back, and the English were as feeble in standing up to Hitler and Mussolini as I had been in rescuing Koestler or unmasking Franco.

I went back to Prague, still trying but failing again to save the Czechs.

The last time Edgar and I were to meet in that compelling era when we all felt part of the battle was in 1940, after the fall of France. We were walking down Piccadilly. Why, I said, did the French surrender?

He pointed to a double-decker bus hurtling down the street. 'Go out and stop that with your bare hands,' he said.

Eventually, of course, we did – with American help. But if Arthur Koestler survived, so did General Franco, and many, many of our friends and allies perished and the lines got tangled up. Not only did Simon die as Otto Katz in Prague but the Czechs themselves were trampled down by Russia when the Germans had been thrown out. But I expect those three young men did all right and are now powerful figures in modern Spain. I never could remember their names.

Derrick Ferguson

AN ARMED SPECTATOR

His Majesty's ships first took me into Spanish waters in the late 1920s when, for instance, Torremolinos was a tiny fishing village and the Costa Brava was almost empty of tourists. Two summer leaves in a villa in Mallorca, staying with my future wife and her parents, greatly enhanced my affection for Spain and Spaniards.

In the summer of 1936 a very different kind of visit unfolded. My ship, H.M.S. *Codrington*, in which I served as flotilla signal officer of the 3rd Destroyer Flotilla, had spent a year in the eastern Mediterranean, applying League of Nations sanctions against Italy in her Abyssinian war. Our flotilla was commissioned on a war basis (after the navy's seventeen years of peace). But on return to our base in Malta, I rented my first married home, which we named Camp de Mar. Then a signal came from the Commander-in-Chief, Mediterranean Fleet: 'Proceed with all despatch to Palma de Mallorca. Further orders follow.'

During my earlier 'Spanish cruises', showing the flag, we had steamed at 'economical speed'; but now 'full speed', thirty knots, was a novelty to the western Mediterranean. On our way we learned that the late governor of the Canaries, General Francisco Franco Bahamonde, had in fact started a civil war against his government, the left-wing government of Spain. It had been a weakening government since the departure of King Alfonso XIII in 1931, ideal for communist undermining. But what on earth had this Franco affair to do with the Royal Navy?

'Further orders' were, in broad terms, to protect British interests; to evacuate British subjects from the war zones and to act with strict neutrality. The last word was of the utmost importance in H.M. Government's policy; but it was the most difficult to implement for His Majesty's ships in Spanish waters.

Even in those days there were some tourists in Mallorca: a few hundred, perhaps, of British and friendly nationalities, but more than a destroyer could evacuate. Fortunately H.M.S. *Repulse* was sent to join us. This large battle cruiser took the lot, except for a delightful old lady, living at Camp de Mar, on the west coast of the island, with her large contingent of dogs. Her husband Cecil Aldin, a famous British dog artist, had died there. The climate, she said, had given him twelve extra years of life; their dogs had given them their living; so she would stay with the dogs in Camp de Mar for the duration.

My captain, Geoffrey Miles (now Admiral Sir Geoffrey Miles, K.C.B., K.C.S.I.), as senior British naval officer in the area, had to find a role: what precisely did neutrality mean and whom should we help and how? We were blessed by one piece of good luck: the honorary British vice-consul in Palma was a retired naval officer, Spanish-speaking and extremely knowledgeable. Lieutenant-Commander Alan Hilgarth had retired with his wife to a charming, manor house style of farm in the hinterland, there peacefully to write books. A small vice-consul's office, with a very small stationery allowance to keep government paper-work going, gave him local status. Little did he know that from the moment of our arrival on the scene, his peaceful authorship was to be eroded, as a life of intense activity was to begin, leading eventually to his promotion and appointment as British Naval Attaché, Madrid, in the Second World War. He was a brilliant man, and, having met him in peacetime, I recommended to my captain the closest possible liaison in finding our role. This contact helped immeasurably during the inevitable confusion of a civil war, in which we had no obvious part to play.

Where should we base ourselves and the ships in our flotilla? This was a problem in itself. The best arrangement appeared to be for us to spend part of the time in the Balearic Islands, which were under General Franco's revolutionary flag, and part of the time along the

Catalan coast, held by the 'Red' government of Spain. In practice, H.M.S. *Codrington,* the flotilla leader, made frequent passages at reasonable intervals between Palma and Barcelona, whilst our other ships visited the lesser ports. We were thus well informed and, above all, could tell the Foreign Secretary, Anthony Eden, in a nightly signal, our precise front-row-of-the-stalls interpretation of events and drama in a fluid and vicious struggle. My signal communications duties brought before my eyes the link, this invaluable link, which we had become between H.M. Government and this war, in which the dictators of Italy and Germany were becoming rapidly embroiled and into which Russia was pouring money to support a proletariat to overthrow Church, State and Establishment, thence to build up a communist dictatorship. Great Britain and France were straining to keep neutral, and we were the local implementation of armed neutrality. The gathering storm, as Winston Churchill so aptly named the era, was just off our quarterdeck. Direct radio communication with the Foreign Secretary, via the Admiralty, became an enthralling duty and my own main personal task: it was the conveyance of thought, rapidly, accurately, and wrapped up in a cloak of cryptography.

An early incident brought home to me the appalling confusion reigning. It concerned a Spanish cruiser on the government side; the ship herself was in a state of communist revolution, although Franco's forces were the 'revolutionaries'. It happened when H.M.S. *Codrington* had gone to Gibraltar to fuel, leaving the flag of British neutrality in north-east Spanish waters in the hands of H.M.S. *Ardent.* We had scarcely had a chance to stretch our legs ashore when I received a signal reporting a British merchant ship (S.S. *Gibel Zerjon II*) being menaced by a Spanish cruiser off Melilla, Spanish Morocco. My captain ordered steam for full speed, and we raced to the reported position at thirty knots to investigate – a potentially tricky problem because the position in the report was only a mile or two beyond twelve miles from the coast. Spain claimed territorial waters up to twelve miles, and although I believe we only recognized the three mile limit, as in United Kingdom waters at that time, this point might be troublesome.

Smoke appeared over the horizon and soon a bulky silhouette was recognized from *Jane's Fighting Ships* as the Spanish cruiser *Miguel de Cervantes*, lying close to a very small coaster, the vessel in our signal, the *Gibel Zerjon*, who plied her regular trade between Gibraltar and Morocco. The flotilla navigator fixed both vessels, and as they were thirteen-and-a-half miles from the nearest coastline the breaking of neutrality was not so far involved.

This looked like a clear case of piracy, but the 'International Code of Signals' contained nothing about pirates, so I first hoisted a simple, single flag signal, Flag 'X', which means 'Stop carrying out your intentions and watch for my signals'. The cruiser answered without undue delay. My next signal from our captain was a rather more complicated hoist of flags: 'Cease Interfering', which, after a long delay, was answered by the Spaniards. Their answering pendant only showed that they had understood the signal, not an indication of complying with it. The cruiser and the vessel, owned by Bland & Co. of Gibraltar, both remained with engines stopped, the *Gibel Zerjon* belching black smoke. Captain Miles decided to board the cruiser, not with an armed boarding party, but with a team of four; he was going himself, with his signal officer (myself), his navigator and the chief coxswain. We dressed in No. 10's (smart white uniform with swords), making the visit partly an official call and partly a boarding at sea. We were lowered in a whaler, and while we were rowed across a second whaler was sent to the merchant ship to hear their story.

The Spaniards lowered a jumping ladder over the ship's side and gave our whaler a bow line as we clambered up: an extremely tense moment, accentuated by the whole ship's company seeming to be gathering around us. They were dressed in motley clothing and most were unshaven; the scene took me back to the days of buccaneers and pirates as there was little sign of any naval uniform. However, to our astonishment, a boatswain's mate, or someone, piped us on board. It is an old naval custom to pipe on board all foreign naval officers in uniform. Facing this un-uniformed, apparently undisciplined mob on deck, the shrill boatswain's call gave us a welcome note of normality.

One of the older men, wearing a petty officer's cap, but otherwise in pirate's rig, allowed us to squeeze through the uncouth crowd and make our way up the ladders to the bridge; he accompanied us there and became our unsure interpreter. With his halting English and my smattering of Spanish, we explained why our captain was on board and asked to see the Spanish captain. Here we met trouble: they had no captain, no navigator, no officer of the watch. The command of *Miguel de Cervantes* rested with a committee of forty men, on or around the bridge: seamen, stokers, cooks and other ratings. They told us that they had shot their officers and, standing in the midst of this pressing crowd on the bridge, we were estimating the odds on our own survival! The friendly petty officer who was vaguely conducting the parley told us that he had done a little small-boat navigation on his courses, and the three ships were on the chart: well inside Spanish waters. Captain by physically pushing through 'The Committee' we eventually reached the chart table in the charthouse, where he showed us where he thought Miles (a navigation specialist before promotion) showed him, for the Committee's benefit, the ships' actual positions: one and a half miles outside Spanish territorial waters. So they dropped that argument and then stated that this British vessel from Gibraltar was gun-running for the revolutionary General Franco, whose soldiers controlled Spanish Morocco. We assured them that she was doing nothing of the kind; she was on her normal trade run, cleared by the British authorities in Gibraltar to proceed on her lawful occasions.

Suddenly the comic side struck me: this once formidable cruiser, now representing the government of Spain with a chaotic, revolutionary crew, was ignorantly trying to wield power against another revolution ashore and was being frustrated on a technicality they did not understand: accurate navigation.

The Committee, personified by their spokesman, accepted our orders to free the British ship. The subsequent phrase, 'Otherwise we will be forced to sink you', may not have been fully understood, for we were then taken on a brief, conducted tour round the ship, tailed by the Committee. We were shown into the ward room, where they pointed out the many gruesome bullet holes: the scene of the murder of their officers. Then, further aft, in the admiral's cabin, we were shown the chair where he had likewise been executed. My impression of this uncomfortable, between-decks tour was that of a naive attempt to prove that they truly had no officers to conduct a parley with us.

By the time we were up on deck again, a large proportion of the ship's company, thronging around the jumping ladder, had put on their uniform caps – as a concession to the smart uniforms of their 'visitors' perhaps – and many of them saluted as we made for the jumping ladder to depart. We were duly piped over the side, leaving a sea of salutes on deck.

It was becoming increasingly difficult for us, the neutral, armed spectators, to comprehend this developing civil war and our proper role in it. The 'revolutionaries' were the smart, well equipped, well led and disciplined forces. The government forces were badly led, ill equipped and apparently undisciplined, yet very strong in fighting spirit. In Barcelona the Catalans were traditionally against the Madrid government, but they supported it now, as a left-wing, almost communist force. We saw the effect, alongside the South Mole in Barcelona harbour, where there was a frequent compulsion to adapt our neutral role to the needs of the moment, especially when we could save lives.

Word had reached the ship in Palma that the lives of a large number of nuns in Barcelona were menaced by the government troops. Death or a worse fate, we were informed, had left fifty survivors, and an unidentified 'local authority' was willing to exchange these hostages for two 'loyal generals' in custody as hostages in Mallorca. The British vice-consul sorted out the details with the aid of a Roman Catholic priest. Armed with the name of a priestly contact in Barcelona, we sailed, with the generals on board.

Barcelona was chaotic when we berthed; sporadic rifle fire came from many directions in the city, and aircraft, understood to be German 'volunteers', had been bombing the night before. A night safety anchorage for neutral vessels had been promulgated, and we were advised to go there before dusk.

It took most of the afternoon to negotiate permission to land, owing to a lack of recognizable authorities, but eventually I was given the task of going ashore to find a disguised R.C. priest, believed to be dwelling somewhere near the port. Luck once more played a part.

I had met, during my peacetime visits to Mallorca, a charming Spanish girl, engaged to a wing-commander in the Spanish air force. She was again on holiday there when the Civil War began; but now she was unable to leave and, with winter approaching, she needed her warmer clothes from her home in Barcelona. So she had given me the name *and address* of her parish priest, with a note for him listing the clothes she wanted the priest to collect from her empty home, pack, and bring in a suitcase to H.M.S. *Codrington*. The name was the same as my nun contact: the same priest, and he was at home in his flat when I called on him.

By dusk we had most of the fifty nuns, all in civilian clothes, of course, trailing on board in twos and threes. One of them stepped over the brow and kept on rubbing her shoes on the gangway mat on the quarterdeck. 'British soil at last,' she exclaimed, literally weeping for joy.

The disposal of the two hostage generals was more difficult, owing to the chaos ashore: no one appeared to be in authority nor could we find anyone interested. I found a kind of sentry on the quay, not in uniform, but armed with a revolver and holster round his waist. I asked who his superior officer was; but my Spanish was not Catalan, so I tried: 'From whom do you get your orders?' His laconic reply summed up the situation only too well, as I remember it. He said, 'From the next man with a pistol.' So we had to turn the generals loose on the jetty, as it was, by then, time to make for the safety anchorage, a few miles away, at full speed.

I went into the ward room for a drink when we had anchored and found a jovial, possibly hilarious nuns' sherry party in progress. A brother officer told me he had thought they all needed 'ginning up a bit', and how right he was. After two or three sherries each, and with their terrible ordeals behind them, they were served with dinner in relays (our mess was only designed for about twelve officers), and we sailed for Mallorca at midnight. Nuns were draped unashamedly along the ward room settees and armchairs, on blankets on the deck and a lucky few in the cabins of officers on duty, all sleeping well.

In the morning an English nun interpreted, over breakfast, the tale of terror during their last few days around Barcelona. 'Now', she said, 'succour had come and their prayers were answered. They were safe on board a British warship.'

The triple terror of this civil war had struck ruthlessly along the Spanish coast: fear of the next man with a pistol, the terror of aerial bombing, and the alarm and horror of coastal bombardment by unidentified black silhouettes in the moonlight. Ships of our flotilla in Tarragona, Valencia, Alicante and Cartagena transmitted to us similar reports for inclusion in our nightly summary to the Foreign Office.

We knew those silhouettes, which ships they were, not only from our excellent Naval Intelligence, but also from periods of recuperation at Tangier, which was then under a form of international control. There, in the garden of the Italian legation, was spread out a network of masts and radio aerials, forming a most undiplomatic communications centre for clandestine naval activity by pro-fascist forces in the western Mediterranean.

The new German pocket battleship *Graf Spee* came into the anchorage for a rest, while we were there. The usual commanding officers' courtesy calls were exchanged, followed by a signal from the German executive officer inviting our ward room officers to come over. We were well entertained in their ward room with quantities of Munich beer followed by 'chasers' of brandy, and were then told that they would be proud to show us round their fine ship. This was a very unexpected offer, all in our favour, as our own ship, if there was a return visit, could show little of interest to them. 'You may go with us anywhere you wish,' the commander said, and off we went on a most informative tour. 'We are your friends,' the commander was at pains to emphasize. 'The German navy, our new navy, will *never* fight the Royal Navy again' – how well I remember the next phrase – 'unless our Fuehrer orders it, but we do not believe that will happen.'

That visit took place when Italo-German naval cooperation in support of General Franco's forces in the Civil War was forging the Rome-Berlin Axis, as it became known.

The *Anschluss* and the trail of subsequent German aggressions led to the doom, five years later, of this magnificent ship, at the Battle of the River Plate. At Tangier we had been drinking with German naval officers on the doorstep of history.

Alfred Lent

THE BLOND MOORS ARE COMING!

GERMAN FLAK GUNNERS IN SPAIN – THE CONDOR LEGION STORY

In January 1938 a detachment of Luftwaffe privates and N.C.O.s, among them this writer, stood at the Hamburg docks ready for embarkation. The smart tailored uniforms had given way to ill-fitting civilian clothes, with our regulation boots sticking out conspicuously from underneath the trouser cuffs. Our destination was Vigo, Spain.

We were about 150 trained soldiers, mostly in our second year of National Service, chosen from various flak and signals regiments to take part in the regular relief for the 'Assignment Rügen': this was a code name for the task force in Spain because the first units had been assembled on that Baltic island. We knew more or less what to expect, although barrack rumours about the German participation in the Spanish Civil War had provided but scanty information.

As a matter of fact, only upon assembly of our group of volunteers did I hear the name Condor Legion mentioned for the first time. I thought it rather fetching until some cynics remarked that this noble bird was actually a vulture. One pleasant surprise during the last briefing, when a somewhat pompous colonel of the Air Ministry had made a farewell speech, was the announcement of our rate of pay, which equalled a manager's salary on civvy street. Nobody had expected such largesse, and the customary three cheers for the Fatherland were delivered with genuine enthusiasm.

At the sight of the harbour, after having walked there as unmilitarily as possible from the main station, we realized how thin our disguise as a 'football club' really was. The waterfront people all seemed very much in on the secret. 'Here comes Max Winkler,' I overheard somebody say. The non-existent Herr Winkler was the postal code name under which the legionaries could receive mail from their families and friends. It was natural for some people to put two and two together, but when street urchins called after us to bring them some Spanish oranges from the pitch I began to wonder about the efficiency of German war secrecy. However, we were soon to learn that the charade of non-intervention could be played more seriously.

A mystery ship

Motor launches, manned by *Kriegsmarine* sailors dressed up as civilian boatmen, ferried us to our ship. Some landlubbers from Württemberg who had never yet seen the sea held on tightly to the railings when the choppy waves of the Elbe estuary rocked the boats, and taunts about 'Franco's Last Stand' seemed quite appropriate.

A couple of miles downstream a small cargo vessel was waiting for us, tucked away in a far-off berth. It was the *Golfo de Darien*, flying the Panamanian flag. This converted freighter carrying shells, spare parts and human cargo soon began a pitching and rolling voyage towards the English Channel. Whenever the seasick tried for a breath of fresh air, it was not long before the boatswain's whistle blew, sending everybody below ('downstairs' some called it). It meant that there was shipping nearby – fishing vessels, ferries, and once we spotted a two-engined aircraft going south. Nobody was allowed on deck at such critical moments. Observation of a small tramp with long rows of human faces uncharacteristically hanging over her sides could not have aroused much more international suspicion if she had been flying the skull and crossbones.

The German navy has always been renowned for good food. Regularly as clockwork, plenty of it was ladled out for us upon the tables set up on the spotlighted platforms under the fore and aft hatches. Some could keep it down and did their best during the dreaded washing up. I saw a man vomit into his cloth cap to avoid hitting the dish water flopping to and fro in the big tubs. Seasickness does not rank highly among the horrors of war, except of course for the afflicted who just want to die. The daily wastage of food could have fed the same number of Spanish soldiers for a week.

At last, nearer to Spanish waters, the Bay of Biscay became unexpectedly calm. Temperatures rose and no ships came into sight. We spent hours on deck, singing the sentimental songs so dear to the Teutonic heart, watching sunsets and once a shark in the ship's wake. We beheld the sinister creature of our sea stories with fascination. Fiction had come true at last.

It must be emphasized that contrary to the general belief we were by no means pressganged into this enterprise. There was no coercion, but unlike the International Brigade, the 'Last of the Idealists', who were encountered later and won our respect, our participation had little or nothing to do with political ideology. Our model was the *Landsknecht*, the colourful, swaggering mercenary from a romantic past. The very name of Spain conveyed glamour and adventure in the tradition of what in Britain would have been regarded as *Boy's Own* paper stuff. A civil war in Russia would have caused much less interest, let alone sufficient enthusiasm to participate in it. Our only concern was that this caper should not exceed our regular date of discharge from the Wehrmacht, and nobody was ever motivated by the expectation of financial gains.

The trip took five days. Homeward bound, three-quarters of a year later, it was even to take nine against strong headwinds. The other shuttle service from Germany to Spain was by air via Majorca and Italy, but this was reserved for the sick and wounded, for top brass and people with good connections, and for the dead.

The war from another century

At Vigo we disembarked in the dark and piled on to the train to Burgos. When the window blinds were raised on a dazzling blue morning over golden mountains, our first sight of Spain was like being in the cinema. The first native soldier we ever saw, with his tasselled cap, a cloak made from a striped blanket and canvas shoes with straw soles, almost looked comical to us pampered members of the Luftwaffe, accustomed to spit and polish and the best of everything. In León I tried to attract the attention of an ice cream vendor from the window. I did not dare leave the train lest it should suddenly move out and leave me stranded. When I beckoned he gave me a funny look. When I beckoned harder he seemed positively hurt, and when I became frantic he shrugged and walked stiffly out of sight. Later I learned that our gestures of 'Come here' and 'Go away' are reversed in Spain.

The first evidence of war and destruction soon came into view, reminding us that this after all was not a package holiday for tourists. Shattered vehicles and burned-out houses were still bearing the crude lettering '*No pasarán*!', the futile promise of the loyalists not to let the enemy pass – heroic, pathetic and on the way out of history into legend.

Burgos, transformed from a sleepy provincial town into the Nationalist capital, resembled a stage production of an operatic war dating back to the Carlists. With its Gothic spires and cypress trees set in the landscape of Old Castile, the place was alive with people and colours. There was the red and gold of Imperial Spain and the white banner of Navarre with its red St Andrew's Cross. Colourful posters promoted the war effort and the bullfights Franco had reintroduced as one of the first amenities in the provinces wrested from the Republic. Girls in mantillas promenaded on the *paseo* in convoys of duennas, peasants with their ubiquitous mules and big-wheeled carts marketed their produce, and townspeople mingled with soldiers of every description. The Moroccan lancers of Franco's bodyguard in white cloaks walked next to Falangists in blue shirts and monarchists in red berets; then there were the Guardia Civil whose black lacquered 'dust shovels' have evolved from the traditional Spanish hat, the rear brim being turned up to make back-to-the-wall fighting easier. They all made it clear that this war was indeed very different from the conventional image.

Smack in the middle of the scene our 'football club' made its star entrance. The Condor Legion's march through history, from my own point of view, began and ended with two parades: the victory march towards the Brandenburg gate, stiffly formal and goose-stepping in 1939, and this improvised one, almost sauntering from Burgos station to our billet in a school building next to the bull ring. The main street to the Plaza Mayor, always the centre of an outdoors social life, was crowded with people welcoming us with applause, a rather pleasant contrast to the 'Heil'-shouting in Germany on similar occasions.

At H.Q. the 'Max Winkler outfits' were replaced by proper brown uniforms, not much to look at but with Spanish insignia always one rank higher than the one held at home. My first visit to town was to a menswear shop, for the purpose of buying a woollen cardigan. The renowned German war machine had fallen flat on the supply of pull-overs, and February in the Spanish highlands holds some icy winds in store.

For several days we were at liberty to mingle with the crowd. A mutual camaraderie existed between ourselves and the regular Moroccan infantry, beturbaned fellows with the blue-grey eyes of their 'Vandalusian' ancestors gleaming in the dark faces of Africa.* To them we were the men who in 1936 had made their legendary trip in Junkers 52 transport planes across the Straits of Gibraltar possible. As a mark of brotherhood they called us 'Moros rubios', the blond Moors, and the salute exchanged was mutually snappy. We in turn respected their fighting qualities, about which many stories were told. That they were disliked even by the Spaniards on their side was no concern of ours.

With a generous allowance in pesetas at our command we explored Burgos, buying souvenirs 'Toledo' style, and sampled Spanish menus and wines in restaurants, of which there was no shortage. To our dismay we found that meals were not served before 9 or even 10 p.m. Because of the siesta in the afternoon social life was extended to the small hours. We followed in the wake of experienced 'rear echelon pigs' among our older comrades to the brothels. To our amusement they were all situated in the immediate vicinity of the thirteenth-century cathedral – a magnificent edifice, built among others by the same German architects who had also worked in Cologne when Western Europe was just called Christendom.

However, as always in a soldier's life, the good days never last long, and when it comes to combat assignments things can move very fast indeed.

Baptism of fire

From the meandering front lines on our maps of Aragon, pencilled arrows sprout towards the Mediterranean, indicating the progress of the March offensive, destined to split Republican Spain in two. In the path of the advancing columns lies the town of Belchite, its first

* The Spanish province of Andalusia got its name from the much maligned Germanic tribe of the Vandals who migrated in the Dark Ages as far as Tunisia.

objective. The four 8.8-cm guns are poised to fire at low angle from an open position next to an olive grove. They stand in kite-shaped formation with three front pieces in action against ground targets. The fourth is waiting for enemy planes that never seem to come. About 200 yards away, connected by electric cables which actuate the controls for anti-aircraft combat, the stereomatic direction finder also remains idle on this day.

I cannot help marvelling at our own vast superiority in numbers and material. Streams of Heinkel 111s, protected by Messerschmitt fighters and alternating with Italian Caproni and Savoia bombers, carry out their missions unopposed but for the occasional twin puffs of smoke from the enemy's double-barrelled French anti-aircraft guns. Some four miles away, the mountains resemble erupting volcanoes from heavy Nationalist gun-fire. Our groups of flak shell bursts are clearly discernible. We are known as one of the 'mad' batteries because of our firing speed and precision.

We never have to worry about the supply of ammunition. One barrel can manage up to 4,000 shots before it becomes dangerously prone to detonation in the bore. On a busy day our battery is able to fire 1,200 rounds before the gunners drop with fatigue at sunset. For the first time in history we are witnessing the miracle of how long the Reds can withstand a barrage. A wireless message from the Nationalist General Aranda, transmitted on our wavelength, has just requested 'Devils' on some road intersection or other. It is the code for the German Stukas.

The long barrels of our guns are like pointers indicating the progress of battle. The higher the elevation, the farther the enemy has been driven back. We should be closing shop soon, as we always do by nightfall in this war. Our chief, with one lieutenant and a wireless crew, is still on his advanced observation post watching the heroic little 'Spaniacs' carrying their battle flags from one mountain top to the next. He corrects our fire from what he sees through a trench telescope. The adjustments made with a protractor on a survey chart are radioed back to the gun-layers. Our 'old' men still remember how they once outgunned a howitzer hidden behind hills, a dreaded adversary because of its steep trajectory.

'The village of Fuendetodos has fallen. For tonight expect Liberty!' Message received. Cheers go up. A code word of alluring sound but meaning hard work, namely a shift of position with all the heavy equipment. According to the map, the advance must have covered close to twenty miles. After the stalemate at Teruel during the recent winter campaign, this is quite extraordinary. We do not pitch tents but prepare to huddle together for a few hours of sleep on the stony ground. The silvery olive branches afford scanty camouflage. Then the traction engines are brought up from the rear to be loaded under cover of a complete blackout. Some bloody Spaniards come tearing along in lorries, exuberantly singing their hymn 'Face towards the Sun', with headlights appropriately on full beam. Foot soldiers arrive and set bonfires ablaze. Attracted by the commotion it does not take long for our nocturnal visitor to appear.

It is an enemy spotter and nuisance plane. We call him the 'Red Ghost', for nobody has ever seen him, or simply the 'coffee-grinder' because of the obsolete sound of the engine. He has soon spotted us in the clear moonlight. For the first time I hear the hissing of falling bombs, soon to become so familiar to city-dwellers all over Europe. We dive for cover in the blinding flash of explosions, but the result is negative. We curse the fact that the searchlights of the Legion, first in action around Seville early in 1937, have long since been withdrawn. The Spaniards are now very busy quenching their bonfires. We curse them too.

The geometry of death

Azaila has fallen. We have bypassed Belchite, a town so devastated that we believe reconstruction to be impossible. The next goal is Caspe at the lower course of the Ebro, just where the loop of the river begins.

It is a morning of chilly mist and a promise of heat later. The low-level raid comes as a complete surprise. The aircraft is not one of the elegant silver-grey with white tail fins and slim diagonal black crosses of our own. It is an ugly Curtiss double-decker snub nose in yellow fabric with the red-gold-mauve colours of the Spanish Republic, sporting wing tips blazing in venomous red. The enemy is strafing the nearby road. We open fire just when he is approaching.

For the first time I am working as a new operator among the eleven crew members of the firing computer. When such a situation is relived later it is customary to say that this was the moment one had been waiting for, but this is a fallacy. A man just becomes an automaton within a complicated technical procedure.

In the few seconds that have elapsed since the alarm was given, we have pivoted the control table and caught the plane on the sights of the long-base rangefinder in order to determine the advance angle of our shot. My own calculating component is a rotary drum with graphic lines for the conversion of distance into height.

It is a geometry of death. My enemy is not the plane overhead, its wings flashing like blood-tipped sword blades in the sky. It is not even the man up there, now pitting his flying skill against our mathematics. My adversary is a tiny cross-spider in the indicator window, constantly trying to escape from its correct course. I have to control it by crank-wheel and force it to follow a network of parabolic lines on its way to the delay corrector, where it will be digested, together with horizontal speed, flight direction and ballistic velocity, and finally end up as firing data on the gunner's control lamps. Stunned by blasts, I seem to shrink until I am no more than a dot on a graphic chart. My body is buffeted by shock waves, my knees tremble, my eyes are smarting from sweat, dust and fumes. We keep firing. 'Smoke trail!' the rangefinder calls out. This is believed to be the tell-tale sign of an imminent crash. Some of our chaps in the rear limber position see fit to shout 'Hurrah!'

Exuberance is cut short. I can hear a muffled explosion in our battery just when the last salvo is delivered while the plane dives to what may be destruction or safety behind a mountain ridge. More smoke. Men are running. The millionth chance has happened.

We fire cartridges which the breech ejects after the shot – like a pistol. At one fatal moment one of them has bounced off the outrigger of the platform and hit a shell basket, carelessly put on the ground with its open lid towards the gun. The impact has exploded the powder charge, showering the crew with metal fragments. Gunner No. 1 got it right in the spine. His dreams of glory are over.

The long hot summer of battle

The seasons of the year have gone by – after three months of winter, nine months of hell, as the Spaniards themselves describe their climate. We have seen the High Pyrenees during the Barbastro campaign and the capture of Tremp with its important power station. We have forded clear streams with their bridges in ruins and fired from precipitous cliffs under the snow-clad Mount Perdido close to the French border. We have taken part in the advance against Castellón de la Plana, when Franco did not do too well along the coast and we had to retreat, later to put in a 'wedge' via Albocacér and the incredible mountain aerie of Morella.

Here I experienced the one and only high-level attack by a large formation of Martin bombers coming straight at us. Under fire, their bombs were jettisoned and badly shook up one of our own light 3.7-cm batteries standing in the front line two miles ahead of us. Neither side achieved a hit. Ten days later came our entry into Castellón, acclaimed by the people emerging from their dugouts. We gave the poor souls all our rations as a gesture of goodwill. To us, it was a highlight of the campaign.

We have also been through the boredom of airstrip protection in the rear. When soldiers have nothing to do, up goes the sick list. Once we were in luck, being detailed to La Cenia near the port of Vinaroz. Our tents stood next to shady fig trees and a cascading brook where we could bathe in a waterfall, but upon another occasion they stood right on the tarmac. It was like the Devil's own frying pan. Innumerable flies swarmed from dawn till dusk and crawled all over us and the food. I went down with a 'Spanish' diarrhoea and spent a week in the field hospital of Saragossa, tended by smiling nuns and enjoying the comfort of being somewhat less hot and fly-infested than in the field.

Meanwhile, the final offensive against Catalonia was in full swing. One more winter of war lay ahead. The enemy's temporary advance across the loop of the Ebro had been stopped, but they kept sending supplies across the river. Their pontoon bridge seemed to be indestructible, in spite of the most intensive bombardment. Our battery joined in and tried to shoot it up Great War-style (not yet known as the First World War), in cooperation with a rather shaky Heinkel 45 as a spotter plane since the target was just out of our range of observation in enemy hinterland. Also, we had to wait for the midday sun to warm up our ammo; heated powder carries the shot farther. The plane kept cruising over the front line and watched our fire, then flew back to drop scribbled notes with corrections attached to smoke cartridges for easy discovery in the fields surrounding our position.

It went on for hours but the target was obviously endowed with a charmed life. In the end, when the pilot had to call it a day, he informed us in a final message: 'Fed up. Going home for dinner. Bridge still intact.' The sarcasm of those 'famous last words' survived in the Luftwaffe for years to come, being quoted whenever something went wrong, long after their origin was forgotten.

I did not stay to see what happened afterwards. The bridge, I learned, became quite famous, but unbeknownst to me this had been my last day in action. 'Hey, boy, it's Alemania for you,' I was greeted with envy after my return from picking up the cartridges and rolling up the telephone wire. My eight months of service in 'Rügen' were over. The relief personnel had arrived. The old *Golfo* was waiting for me in Vigo – and a hero's welcome at home.

Kenneth Sinclair-Loutit

THE LARGEST FRYING PAN IN THE WORLD

We were in Grañen – outside Huesca, which was in fascist hands – because Peter Spencer (he kept his identity as Viscount Churchill in reserve for its use in P.R. where it would count better than in Spain) had looked at the Michelin map and said that Grañen was the only place that drained the whole front *and* gave two ways back if we had to move. Peter had made this choice in Barcelona on Brigade of Guards' criteria, not taking account of the fact that Grañen was an anarchist village, and that an F.A.I. activist with the *nom de guerre* of Pancho Villa was the undisputed chief of all that happened there.

Pancho Villa was a fat, hardy peasant, who had had a tiny *tienda* in Lerida where he sold beans, chickpeas, salt and flour to those even poorer than himself. He was physically strong, and morally resentful of his poverty, perhaps because his Aragonese pride was hurt every time his Catalan wholesaler refused him stock before the last was paid for. In the end he was thrown out of his shop, and as a lifelong member of the F.A.I. he was kept alive by his *compañeros*. In July 1936 he came alive and arrived in a commandeered truck in Grañen to put an end to the exploitation of man by man and to end the poison of private property. He wore a black hat and a red handkerchief around his neck, and always carried a large pistol in an unstrapped holster. He was not a thug. He could laugh and did so mightily, and he cultivated the toughness that anarchists seemed to believe necessary to distinguish themselves from namby-pamby communists. Pancho Villa always had a three-day beard, and he drank from the bottle, which did not touch his lips; for elegance he used a *porrón*, and when pleased he would play with the jet, seeking out the dry patches in his mouth.

Pancho Villa had not been consulted, and when we arrived in Grañen he saw in the British Medical Unit the advance guard of that most vicious thing – centralized interference with personal liberty. Since we had our own stores he could not starve us out, but he astutely saw our dependence on motor fuel, and confiscated our entire stock. War was declared, one of those sub-conflicts that made it hard to see between whom the real Civil War was being fought. The inflammable nature of the *casus belli* saved us, because Pancho Villa, who never stopped smoking, set fire to our petrol and burned himself quite badly.

The first we knew of it was the arrival of Pancho Villa's bodyguard. The Negus (the nimble gypsy who was on duty at the entrance of our farmhouse hospital) came belting into the room where we were on stand-by shouting that the hospital was being attacked. In a sense it was, as Pancho Villa's henchmen had come to ensure that their burned boss would be properly received.

We looked after the singed anarchist as though he was the only person that mattered. In fact we tried to do exactly this with all casualties; as the Huesca front was very quiet in November 1936 we were able, on that day, to give a standard of bedside care to Pancho of positively bourgeois dimensions. Our nurses looked charmingly Miss Nightingale in their starched uniforms, and Pancho Villa was quite literally eating out of their hands, and settled down to purr like a big pussy cat. After that we had no more trouble from the F.A.I. in Grañen, and when Pancho Villa eventually tore himself reluctantly away from the tender loving care of our hospital he decided to give us a treat, and got in touch with the militia of the Gastronomic Workers' Union, which united the syndicalist aspirations of the Barcelona catering trades.

All unions had replied to the call to resist the military revolt, and in the beginning the front lines were manned by centuria of people's militia which were quite simply composed of trade union branch meetings that had been issued with arms (or sometimes not), and had marched off towards the nearest fascist strongpoint. Wherever the two sides met became the front – whether it was sierra or a Madrid suburban apartment house.

Specialized units sometimes put their trade skills at the disposal of the army – an obvious case being that of the hospital workers. The gastronomic workers set up field kitchens, and really tried to feed those who were fighting better than they would have been fed had they stayed at the factory bench or on the farm. It was in this spirit that Pancho Villa's friends had invented and made (with the help of anarchist metal workers) the biggest frying pan in the world.

It was about ten feet in diameter and must have had about sixteen handles in the form of loops of metal, each under the control of one man. The chief cook operated a great wooden paddle, and the only dish ever attempted was a gargantuan paella.

I remember going one evening, at Pancho Villa's invitation, to a small village where the whole population had made a bonfire as wide as the pan. The fire was not burning well, and the chief cook would not unload the pan from its truck until he was satisfied that the fire was of the required standard. Eventually he gave the word, and sixteen men staggered forward with the monstrous iron disc and dumped it in the middle of the conflagration. It was evening, and whatever the fascist garrison of Huesca observed they must have thought it was working in their favour as they did not make any move with their guns. Anyway, anarchists were never concerned with personal security for themselves or others, and they seemed to view death without very much disapproval – it was bad form in the anarchist sectors to suggest that any cover should be used while stopping to talk. Their attitude to machine-gun fire was that of a matador to a bull at five in the afternoon.

The frying pan in position, a whole barrel of oil was poured in, and the neighbourhood became perfumed with the scent of its heating. Then four or five sacks of rice were added, two men holding a sack while a third slit its belly. This produced an audience reaction: there were some gasps, maybe a small cheer. The wooden paddle was worked through the mass, and a sort of golden concrete started to sizzle. Then baskets of onions and buckets of pimentos and tomatoes started a wave of participation, which was let loose by the sacrifice of two sheep – they were dealt with as were the rice sacks: they were disembowelled, skinned and jointed, and in the pan in what seemed like a second. The only light was the flames. The whole affair hung poised very close to the sinister, and as so often at that time, it seemed that I was caught in a *déjà vu*, that I was inside a forgotten Goya, that one of the disasters of war was engulfing me.

Aragon farmhouses are vast and austere, combining barn, cow byre and human habitation. There were about five such houses around an empty space, dust bowl in summer, mud pond in winter. At one end was a ruined chapel which had not been repaired after a fire remembered only by grandfathers. The barns above the cow byres, six feet above the ground, were a natural grandstand. By the light of the fire we could see the flickering white of faces in them. These were the women and children, keeping their distance because the plaza was a man's place. There were some broken carts and our vehicle at the end near the chapel. Suddenly out of the chapel came a prancing figure making a noise like a priest chanting. There was total silence and then with amazing violence Pancho Villa shouted and the man stopped. It was the Negus – whose gypsy gift for the comic was not always deft. Pancho Villa was in no mood to be upstaged. This was a F.A.I. evening; it was in a way his statement of war aims. Meat for everyone always and wine to go with it.

At this moment the chief cook spoke; he said that the fruits of the earth belonged to those who tilled it, that no one would ever be hungry again when Spain was free. He called for more tomatoes and more pimentos, for *ajo* and for water. He orchestrated a veritable potlatch of the village's resources, and himself unloaded a barrel of wine from the truck. Chickens joined the sheep, a small goat went in: every time something was added there was a cheer. The nearby line was abandoned, the sixteen men seized the sixteen handles and shook the pan. The whole area for a mile around must have smelt that paella.

Everyone went to bed in the end gorged. In 1936 that was a very rare feeling in Aragon; indeed, the way things went that may have been the first and last time that many of those there were to eat to repletion.

K. P. Bond

LETTER FROM A REVOLUTIONARY

c/o S.R.I.
Plaza Del Altazano
Barcelona

July 11, 1938

Dear Comrades,

Just a line to show that I have not forgotten comrades of Bromley, in fact I often think of the time I was in England and the time or hours that I could have put in Party work. If I was back I should do these things as much as I did before I came out here for I realise the importance of smashing the Chamberlain government and getting arms for Spain. Also of waking the working class up from their Slumbers. I have not much news, except I have left the place that I first stopped at and am now well the other side of Barcelona and may move on again at any time. Some of the boys that I have met don't have any too good tales to tell of their experiences. They have had to go through a hell of a time because of the Chamberlain government and the backwardness of the English mass movement. I don't mean the C.P. of course.

We got to this place late at night two nights ago, we slept under trees and the next day we made a bit of a hut but the rain got right through it. In fact when I woke I was lying in a pool of water . . .

We do not get much that we can write about, at least I am not a good one to write about things but if I get home I will have plenty to talk about. I have not yet heard from anyone in England and I'm looking forward to some news. I have not learned Spanish yet, it takes a long time to learn anything and not long to forget everything I've learnt. All the boys are OK except they miss their cigarettes, some of them have been smoking coffee and onion leaves, they tried to get me to have a smoke but one pull was enough and you tasted burnt onion for a long time afterwards.

I could do with an English dinner like we had at home, still things are not as bad as they might be. I've broken my belt and had to fix it up with some wire. How's the branch going, have you all been able to settle down and turn Bromley red. I hope you are on the way for the working class must have their brains cleared or the rust cleaned off.

Well I hope it will not be long before the workers of the world gain control of the law, machines, factories and all for the benefit of the community as a whole. Until then we must work and never tire.

I have not anything else to write about of interest, except will Comrade Belsey get any letters that are for me at home and send them on to this address. I don't want my mother to know I'm here for she'll be losing all her sleep worrying.

Well, salud for red Bromley and red England. Salute to the workers that work for the benefit of the workers and the Community as a whole.

K. P. BOND

NOTE ON KENNETH BOND

by H. J. Belsey

Kenneth Bond was born in 1915, in the West Country so far as I remember. In 1936, when I first met him, he was living with his parents at Hayes, Kent, and working as a farm labourer. He was a man of great strength, to whom physical fitness was something very important, and almost indefatigable. After working on the farm for ten hours a day, he would devote three or four hours each evening to his political work.

He had a passionate devotion to socialism. He first joined the Labour League of Youth, in those days an active and militant organization.

In 1936 he was one of half a dozen who founded the Bromley branch of the Communist Party. From the beginning he threw himself into all its activities with a tremendous enthusiasm, taking part in all the big demonstrations of those days, canvassing, selling the *Daily Worker* on the streets. He found time to play an active part in the Cooperative movement and the Transport & General Workers' Union, and to serve for two years as chairman of the Bromley Council Tenants' Association. He read extensively – Marx, Engels and Lenin above all, but he also admired Jack London and Geoffrey Trease.

Finally, the Spanish Republican cause absorbed most of his tireless energy. He did his full share of the routine work, organizing meetings, selling pamphlets, and collecting funds for relief and medical aid. As the war developed, he became more and more determined to go to Spain to fight for what he believed in. Early in 1938 he was accepted for the British Battalion of the International Brigade, and left for Barcelona, where he spent five months in training. At last, in July, he left for the front, and, a few days later, on 28 July, he was killed in action in the successful Ebro offensive.

J. R. Jump

INTERNATIONAL BRIGADER 1

Of the 2,000 men who went from the British Isles to help the Spanish Republic in its fight against the rebel army led by General Franco, about a quarter were killed. Of those who returned to Britain in December 1938 about 200 are still alive.

I was twenty-one when I went to Paris on a day-return ticket, travelled by train to the south of France without a passport and climbed over the Pyrenees at night. Once in Spain, I enlisted in the Spanish People's Army, as it was called, and was drafted into one of the International Brigades.

I was a newspaper reporter and already knew Spanish. Because of this I was given a variety of jobs in the army. After training as a rifleman and then as a machine-gunner, I was clerk-translator and, later, paymaster at the Training Camp headquarters in Tarazona de la Mancha, records clerk at the International Brigades' headquarters in Albacete and, on joining the British Battalion at the front, clerk-interpreter to the Machine Gun Company.

The men with whom I came into contact included miners, shipyard workers, sailors, students, shop assistants, clerks, waiters and former members of the British army and the R.A.F. I remember two Labour councillors, three poets and one author. Many volunteers were members of the Communist Party; some were members of the Labour Party; a number of the Irish were members of the I.R.A.

Though the vast majority had strong political convictions, there were some exceptions. Joe Moran, a Lancashire waiter, told me in France that he was going to Spain to fight against 'Franco and his bloody communists'. John Smith from Glasgow confessed to me that he had volunteered to fight in Spain for three things – drink, women and loot – and had not found much of any. He was killed in the Ebro offensive shortly after being mentioned in dispatches for bravery.

Another man who, I suspect, had no very strong political views when he left Britain was a deserter from the Household Cavalry. He was a New Zealander named Vaughan – though in Spain he adopted the name Van Orren.

The four closest friends I made in Spain were George Jackson, a Cowdenbeath coalminer, Bill Harrington, who had been kicked out of the R.A.F., Dave Newman, a clerk in the employ of Edmonton Town Council, and Jesús Poveda who worked for the town council of Orihuela, Murcia. George was killed in the fighting that followed our crossing of the River Ebro in July 1938. Bill was wounded in the same battle. Dave Newman was invalided out after catching typhoid. Jesús Poveda, a talented poet, fled to France at the end of the war and the last news I had of him was that he was interned at St Cyprien.

When I look at the few faded photographs I brought back with me I remember faces and names that I thought I had forgotten, and recall the good and bad (mostly bad) times we had.

We were a shabby, disreputable-looking lot. Even the new recruits in the training camp at Tarazona de la Mancha near Albacete wore a strange assortment of clothing. Most had khaki shirts, but there was nothing uniform about the rest of our clothes. I had a pair of khaki drill slacks; others had baggy trousers that buttoned at the ankle; a few had knee-breeches and puttees or high leather boots. As I had arrived at the beginning of November I had been issued with a poncho, which could be used at night as an extra blanket. Not so lucky were the men who had been given greatcoats. We wore an assortment of headgear, khaki or black berets, peaked caps and glengarry-type caps. A few had steel helmets. Even in the front line only about one per cent of the soldiers had steel helmets.

This lack of uniformity left the individual free to add or substitute articles of clothing of his own choice. A Californian arranged for a local tailor to make him a cape – rather like an opera cloak, but of khaki woollen material with a red lining. During the short cold winter in la Mancha I used to wear over my shirt a grey hand-knitted cardigan that I had received from England. A friend of mine had a made-to-measure uniform of chocolate-brown corduroy.

Coloured scarves were sported by many Spaniards – red for socialists and communists, red and black for anarchists. There were no regulations against the wearing of political badges. After all, the army had only recently been welded out of the original trade union militias and political units that had come into being after the start of the military rebellion which sparked off the war. We were, however, warned to remove all political badges before going to the front, so that we should not be victims of special persecution if we were taken prisoner. For the same reason some details in our International Brigade *carnets* were never filled in correctly. Everyone, whether student, coalminer, newspaper reporter or clerk, was described as *obrero* (worker), and his politics were entered vaguely as *antifascista.*

The emblem of the International Brigades was a red three-pointed star, in shape not unlike the badge on the bonnet of a Mercedes Benz car. This was worn on the beret or cap, but many Brigaders were never issued with badges.

Instead of, or in addition to, the I.B. emblem, many chose to wear other badges to show their political allegiance, and at the weekly market in the main square of Tarazona there was a good trade in hammer and sickle pins, badges of *Socorro Rojo Internacional* and *Amigos de la Unión Soviética*, and medallions bearing the face of Lenin. There was no personality cult of Spanish politicians, though there was a photograph of President Azaña in every public building.

Alpargatas (canvas shoes with rope soles) were cheap to buy (15p–20p a pair at the official rate of exchange), and like many soldiers I wore them for most of the time except during very cold weather.

On parade, marching through the dusty streets of Tarazona to and from the dining hall or the firing ranges, we bent our elbows and swung our arms across our chests in the Spanish fashion instead of keeping the arms straight as I was later taught in the British army. Our salute was the clenched fist raised to the right temple, but we did not often salute except each morning at the flag-raising ceremony in the main square.

Early in 1938 an attempt was made to enforce a stricter code of military discipline and we were exhorted to salute all officers. There was a noticeable change in many Spanish units of the army, but in the International Brigades nobody took much notice. We continued to call our officers '*Camarada*' unless we knew their christian names. Off duty there was no gulf between officers and men. This camaraderie was even more apparent in the front line where everything was shared – food, tobacco and danger.

Like soldiers everywhere, we complained. We beefed about sleeping on the bare floor of our Tarazona barracks, with only a thin straw palliasse and one blanket to keep out the cold. We moaned about the monotony of the food and the shortage of cigarettes.

I joined the British Battalion in May 1938, after being stationed in Tarazona, Albacete and Vilaseca (Tarragona). The British Battalion of the 15th International Brigade was, like all units of the International Brigades, made up partly of Spaniards – young conscripts. Most companies were mixed, but there was one rifle company that was 100 per cent Spanish until I was posted to it by mistake! It took about a week for the mistake to come to light and be rectified. I was then transferred to the Machine Gun Company as clerk and interpreter.

All companies had a dual command – a commanding officer and a political commissar. The C.O. was responsible for all purely military matters while the commissar looked after the welfare of the men. In practice they always worked together.

While we were training at Tarazona we thought that the life was a hard one. When we joined the battalion we found out that we had been living in comparative luxury. From then on we all slept in the open, except for a few energetic men who dug caves or constructed huts out of canes and branches. In the front line we often suffered hunger and thirst. Worst of all was having to put up with flies, fleas and lice.

The Spanish breed of fly is much more persistent than the English fly. In Spain a fly will settle on, say, your hand. You scare it away, but a second later it settles on exactly the same spot. It does this again and again, never tiring. There were flies everywhere, attracted, no doubt, by the mules and the sickly sweet smell of blood and putrefaction.

Worse than the flies and the fleas were the lice. Unlike the flea, the body louse is a slow-moving creature, and the inexperienced and never-before-bitten might well imagine that it would be easy to kill them.

Individuals could be killed by 'popping' between thumb nails, but what the louse loses by its slowness it over-compensates for by rapid breeding. No matter how many we killed in a delousing session – the main pastime between battles – there were always more to take their place. In the end we just gave up the struggle against the lice and scratched!

When I arrived in Spain our pay was six pesetas a day. Spanish soldiers received ten pesetas. There was an artificial exchange rate of forty pesetas to a pound. Our £1.50 every ten days would purchase very little, for the simple reason that there was little to be bought, except fruit and wine. At the end of 1937 the private's pay was increased to ten pesetas a day. I used to spend it mostly on stationery, stamps, books (which were cheap), newspapers, fruit and drink. For smoking we depended on cigarettes or cigarette tobacco issued to us every week or so. Usually the ration was twenty American (Lucky Strike, Raleigh or Camel), French (Gauloises) or Spanish (Imperiales or Ideales). We did not like the Spanish cigarettes. The tobacco was harsh, and I recalled that a Spaniard had once told me that they were nicknamed *mataquintos* (recruit-killers).

The onset of really hot weather in May gave some of the men the idea of converting their slacks into shorts. I don't know who was the first to do this, but the fashion was followed by both British and Spaniards. We used to go shirtless during the day and only covered the upper part of our bodies after the sun set and the air became chill. This also reduced the lice, as there were fewer places where they could hide. Bare from the waist many became as swarthy as gypsies.

Despite the conditions under which we lived, our discipline was good, though it was seldom imposed from above or, if it was, it was so skilfully done as to be hardly noticed. I never remember any fights breaking out among the men. Perhaps this was because there was little drunkenness, although wine and spirits were very cheap. There was, in fact, an almost puritan attitude to drink and sex.

To be drunk or to catch venereal disease was looked upon as a serious offence, as it weakened not just the individual but the army itself. Both these acts were often compared with self-inflicted wounds or injury through gross carelessness.

There were, of course, some men who wanted to drink. This was appreciated by the political commissars who devised plans which enabled these men to spend their pay on *vino* without overstepping the mark. In my company, when we were stationed behind the lines, C.O. Jack Nalty and Commissar Tom Murray arranged for men to go to the nearest village in pairs, one known drinker with one who could be relied upon not to drink too much, and to see that his comrade did not either. I often went with a Glaswegian. He would drink red wine almost as though it were beer, but never gave me any trouble. When I thought he had had enough, he would walk back to camp with me in a state of exuberance, singing 'I Belong to Glasgow' in the blackness of the night.

An even more serious offence in the International Brigades was racism, but there was little evidence of this. The British Battalion contained many members of the Irish Republican Army and there were also a number of Jews, mainly from Manchester, Leeds and London. In the Washington-Lincoln Battalion there were Jews and Negroes. In the Canadian Mackenzie-Papineau Battalion there were French Canadians and Finns. In the International Brigades all were equal, and I seldom came across any serious friction between men of different race or nationality.

On one occasion I was called in to attend the 'trial' of an Englishman who, in an argument, called a companion 'a dirty, stinking Yid', or words to that effect. The accused and his accuser, Jack Nalty, Tom Murray and I sat cross-legged in a circle. We listened to the complaint. The accused admitted saying the words but declared that he had done so in the heat of the moment. Jack and Tom 'sentenced' him to make an apology. The two men shook hands and went off smoking one of Tom's cigarettes. Tom was a non-smoker but always seemed to have cigarettes for moments like this.

There were, of course, some bad elements. There was one young man with whom I had travelled to Spain. After a few days in Tarazona I never saw him again until the day before we were repatriated. I spoke to him, but I could get no clear account of how he had spent his time in Spain. He said he had been attached to a Spanish unit. Later, I was told that he had been in prison and in a labour battalion. If it was true, I have no idea what his offence was.

Then there was Vicente Terol, a Catalan with whom I had worked for a while in the Record Office. When we joined the Battalion he was drafted into the Spanish Company. I used to see him from time to time, but after a couple of months I missed him and made enquiries.

It was difficult to obtain any information but finally I was told that he had been sent to prison for homosexual activities.

There were occasionally more serious crimes and even the death sentence was imposed on a few occasions.

In April 1938, shortly after the fascist troops reached the Mediterranean, thus driving a wedge between Catalonia and the rest of the Republic, I was called upon to interpret an announcement that was to be made to all the troops. The men assembled on an open heath and a senior Spanish officer stood on a low stone wall to make his speech. After each sentence he paused, so that I could translate. He told us of two members of the International Brigades – they were Scandinavians – who, during the enemy's offensive, had deserted and fled. They had been arrested and at first they had denied that they were soldiers. They had been tried by court martial for cowardice, desertion and Trotskyism and sentenced to death. The sentence had been carried out the same day.

As I translated I could see the sea of upturned faces gazing at the officer and me. All the men were listening intently, but their faces were expressionless. When they were finally dismissed they did not walk away immediately but stood there, still staring, as though they could not believe what they had heard. Eventually, talking quietly in small groups, they dispersed.

We had heard the word 'Trotskyist' many times. It was synonymous with 'defeatist' or 'fascist'. A Trotskyist was one who claimed to be anti-fascist but, because he did not accept the current political 'line' of the Republican government, was in fact said to be helping Franco by destroying the unity of the Republicans. This logic we accepted, for how were we to know anything different? This was the 'line' of all newspapers in Republican Spain and the English newspapers that we read most frequently, the *Daily Worker* and the *News Chronicle*.

The commissar's work, looking after the welfare of the men, was not confined to seeing that the meals were good. They were responsible for education as well. Whenever circumstances permitted, the afternoons were devoted to cultural or political activities. This was not mere indoctrination, though Communist Party policy was often propounded. Many activities were purely educational.

Among the Spanish conscripts there were many who were completely illiterate. They were mostly village lads who had never had a chance to be educated. The commissar arranged literacy classes for these men, and Jesús Poveda was one of the teachers. The pupils were keen and learned quickly – not so difficult in Spanish which is a much more phonetic language than English. There were a few Spaniards who decided that they would like to study English. Classes were arranged for them, and also for the few English who wished to learn Spanish. I used to take one of these classes. It was difficult work, as the educational standards and the ability of the men covered a very wide range. Furthermore, we had neither blackboard nor exercise books, though some men bought copies of a little grammar published by the 15th Brigade. It contained translation exercises like 'Keep your rifle clean. It is your best friend'.

Sometimes there were discussion groups. Often a brigader who had some specialized knowledge would be invited to give a talk and lead a discussion. On one occasion I talked about the British press and a reporter's life. On other afternoons I listened to a Welshman explaining dialectical materialism, an I.R.A. man who gave us a potted history of Ireland, and a trade unionist who spoke about the General Strike of 1926.

When we were in action there was no time for education and the commissar devoted most of his time to looking after the welfare of the men. At meal times, i.e. whenever the kitchen staff could reach us with the huge metal containers of beans, rice, chickpeas or lentils, it was the commissar who arranged for food to be sent to the machine-gun positions. It was his task also to arrange the fair distribution of cigarettes whenever there was an 'issue', and to see that we received letters and parcels promptly. The commissar also kept a company diary of day-to-day events, including a record of casualties.

One day, during a lull in the shelling and bombing of our positions, I was trying to catch a few minutes' sleep when Tom Murray called me over. He handed me a writing pad.

'Do you think they're all right, comrade?' he asked.

He had been writing out half a dozen citations. The names included Jack Nalty, John ('wine, women and loot') Smith, Paddy Duff (company adjutant) and my friend George Jackson. All were commended for bravery in the battles of the previous week, when we had launched attack after attack on a fascist stronghold, Hill 481.

I said I thought the commendations were well deserved and returned the pad to him. Little did I guess that Tom intended to add another name – my own.

This account would be incomplete without a mention of the women in the International Brigades. Most soldiers never came into contact with them, for they were the nurses and sometimes ambulance drivers. I met some of them when I went to hospital in September 1938 shortly before the Spanish government announced that it intended to repatriate all foreign volunteers in the army.

Perhaps the Cabinet imagined that this action, carried out by the League of Nations, would shame Hitler and Mussolini into withdrawing their troops. If so, it was a miscalculation. The Italians and Germans remained and, three months after the International Brigades were disbanded, the war ended.

T. A. R. Hyndman

INTERNATIONAL BRIGADER 2

I was in Portugal with my employer, a journalist, when the Popular Front took over in Spain. We had planned to leave for Greece and on our way stayed in Madrid for a week. There was considerable tension. Some newspapers predicted an uprising by the army. In the Puerta del Sol, on several cold evenings, we were stopped by the Civil Guard. Passports were examined; after protests, a warning was given. We should not keep our hands out of sight, in our coat pockets. We bought gloves.

On a Greek island a book for the Left Book Club was completed. We returned to London for its publication. It did well. My employer, whom I called Stephen, joined the Communist Party which, aided by the left wing of the labour movement, controlled the main thrust of the Popular Front against fascism. I joined also. The vital issue was Spain. A group of British volunteers were already fighting there, including John Cornford and Esmond Romilly. All our spare time was taken up by this cause – marches, rallies, meetings, selling the *Daily Worker* in the streets of London. I noticed that Stephen always returned from meetings with the intellectuals of the party in a slight state of irritation.

Esmond returned from Spain on a recruiting mission. Casualties had been heavy; volunteers were needed, many of them. There was a plan to form a British Battalion of an International Brigade. Esmond, nephew of Winston Churchill, was in the news, the man for the job. He was hardly eighteen years old. John Cornford was reported killed in action. He became symbolic of all we believed in: a poet, romantic, young, a hero.

During all the activities I met Giles, Esmond's brother. He was up at Oxford and hated it. We became friends, and whenever he was in London we met. Not quite so forceful as Esmond, he was, I am sure, a very lonely young man. He telephoned me from Oxford. By some arrangement he was going to leave, for the time being – or something like that. However, the main reason for the call was Spain. Should we join the International Brigade? All over the country hundreds were being enrolled. I arranged to meet him in Hyde Park the next day.

We walked slowly along the main footpath. I told him I would go with him as soon as possible, that once decided it was fatal to hang around, letting friends and families intervene. He had already joined the Communist Party in Oxford; our passports were up to date. He became elated, in full flight. This was a different Giles. 'They will take us on. I have been trained in an O.T.C., you are an ex-Guardsman. Both of us can now fight in a militia. We shall have the right to question any orders with which we don't agree.' He shook his fist at Mayfair where his mother was playing bridge.

I got Giles to move on. A small crowd was collecting. We were not far from Speaker's Corner. We went to his home for tea. Mrs Romilly arrived by taxi. I knew her quite well, and liked her. She changed her gown. Fresh tea was served. Giles told her of our plans. She lit a cigarette, sipped her tea, staring above our heads. Mrs Romilly had an engaging sense of drama, of theatre. 'Two sons,' she said. 'Both in the same war. I must speak to the Colonel.'

She reached for the telephone. 'My father,' said Giles. 'He lives in the country, for health reasons. Have some more walnut cake.' His mother was now listening to her husband. 'Yes, my dear. Of course. You are quite right. I will tell Giles, and his friend. He was in the Guards, you know. No; I don't think he was an officer. See you next weekend. My dear, goodbye.' Mrs Romilly turned to us. 'The Colonel has given me a message for both of you. As soon as you have been accepted, you must both go to the Army and Navy, get yourselves well kitted out with the best boots they have, besides a good supply of their warmest underwear. All on his account. Please do as he says. He is an old soldier. You have his blessing. Now wait a moment.' She went upstairs and came down with the longest scarf I have ever seen. She gave it to me. 'I knitted this myself, for my husband during the war. It is to be worn next to your skin, around your stomach, to keep you warm.' She gave me a kiss. 'Now, some sherry.'

The party recruiting office was crowded. Giles and I were soon accepted, but others were an obvious puzzle. Plenty of enthusiasm but hardly one who could fire a weapon. All were taken on. They would be taught. I had a strange meeting with Bert Overton, who had been a close friend of mine in the Guards. I had not seen him for nearly four years. He had been a brilliant Guardsman, but that was in peacetime. However, he still looked the part. Over some tea in a Lyons we talked of our army days, and now Spain. It did not seem to me that Bert's political motives amounted to much; there were personal reasons, but that could be said of any of us. We agreed to meet in Paris. The night before I left, all I owned was stacked away, my pack was ready. I was Romilly shod, lined, and belly-banded. After some protests, Stephen was very quiet, writing. He was resigned. I was scared. Why and what the hell was I doing?

At Victoria Station the next morning, there was a small crowd to see us off. Mrs Romilly, Communist Party friends, Oxford friends, my family. Stephen handed me thirty one-pound notes, in case, he said, I changed my mind and wanted to get back home. Then the whistle went. The train moved. We hung out of the windows, fists clenched. 'Viva España!' All clenched fists now, including Nellie Romilly, fur-coated. Some heads were high, some were down. Press cameras flashed.

Paris now, and a 'certain address' for another ticket for Perpignan, with food, smokes and cash for the journey. We linked up with Bert. Quietly, I answered Bert's questions on the politics and ideology of the Civil War. He said he understood and agreed. We ate our food, drank a lot of wine, and slept. Suddenly, there was Perpignan. We were met by French communists who checked our names and loaded us into trucks. Altogether we made a total of about forty men. A proper meal at a field kitchen, then darkness. A coach arrived; we stumbled in. The coach began to climb, very slowly. No smoking. No talking. High up in the Pyrenees came the French frontier. We sat very still. The driver produced a list of names, all Spanish, I learned. Over the Spanish frontier. We could talk and smoke. On to Figueras, where we slept for the night in what might have been a church. Anyway, it was now a shelter for men on straw, field kitchens and trucks. The next day came Barcelona, then a train to Albacete, International Brigade headquarters. Finally trucks to Madrigueras, the village a few miles out which was to be our training ground before going into action. A tall young man approached us and checked our names. He then sorted out Giles and myself and said, 'I've been here for two weeks. My name is John Lepper. Welcome to the biggest shambles in Europe.'

John was a liberal anti-fascist. Although the Popular Front included liberals, he had had some difficulties with the communists over getting to Spain. A product of a public school and O.T.C., he could fire a rifle, a pistol, even machine-guns. He told me that he had met a Conservative who had got to Spain with the perfectly logical reason that since the Nazis and Italian fascists would have to be destroyed one day, he might as well start now. The Communist Party had been somewhat suspicious of him, so he joined the Anarcho-Syndicalists, who liked him. The last John heard of him, he was fighting successful battles on the front near Catalonia with the F.A.I. We were all placed in billets for sleeping, and the local church, the largest building in the village, was used as a communal eating place for the villagers and troops. It was all arranged very well by a committee made up from a few workmen and peasants. I was told that about half of the people of Madrigueras had moved out during the early days of the uprising. There had been many executions of leading socialists by Spanish army officers. With fresh volunteers arriving almost every day, the British Battalion was now several hundred strong. By February, with the arrival of a large group of Irishmen, we were almost a complete unit of 400 men. Yet no rifles were issued. At first our commander was Wilfred Macartney. He left under a cloud, literally – of gunpowder. There was a shooting accident in a hotel room in Albacete. Now came Tom Wintringham, almost a founder member of the British Communist Party. He was the man we needed. It took him only a few days to win the respect and loyalty of all under his command. He was cool, quick in deciding who did what, with a wry sense of humour. He took us into action when our turn came.

Giles worked in the orderly room with John Lepper. I called in to talk to them often. 'I wonder what happened to that militia we heard about,' I said. 'There is no such thing around here,' said John. 'A reasonable commander is the best we can expect, and we now have one.' He told Giles that if he still wanted to fight in a militia he should join the anarchists, the ones in the red and black. He had got to know them well in Barcelona, and they fascinated him. When he asked them who gave the orders they said, 'Nobody. We know what to do.' Since all ranks dressed alike, how could they pick out the men in charge? 'No trouble about that,' was the F.A.I. answer. 'We can tell by the looks on their faces.' Some carried guitars only. 'We can't shoot guns, some of us, so we play and sing Flamencos. It scares the shit out of the fascists. They've never heard anything like it.' Until now, neither had we.

Suddenly there were rumours. There was a big push near Madrid. The fascists had to be stopped; their objective was control of the Valley of Jarama: if they succeeded, the capital – still open – could be surrounded, engulfed, cut off. We were issued with rifles and uniforms; I left my civilian clothing with a friendly little family near my billet. Their mother wept. I left her kneeling before her tiny, chipped madonna. All our arms were Russian. They looked good. Any oil, or grease? All in good time, comrade. Trucks, trains, then more trucks. We were there. This battle and its many disasters, terrors and heroism has been described elsewhere by myself and many others. One thing I know. The heavy losses of the first day's fighting could have been avoided. The machine-gun coverage was missing. By early afternoon the lorry which carried them was found. It had overturned. The only way to reach it was to go quickly down a pathway, and drag the guns and ammunition boxes across two sloping ploughed fields, the shortest way. I was glad to be called upon for this rescue job. My rifle was useless, even dangerous, without oil. It could blow up in my face. The enemy fire was increasing. Dive-gunning planes swooped on us. The dead and wounded were everywhere. No stretchers, no food, no water. Most of us got to the guns. Any casualties on our way had to be left; time was precious. I reckon there were about a dozen guns. It is hard to remember exactly. I know they were on small metal wheels, and each gun had a red star. Each man in our team used one hand for his side of a gun, the other hand for a case of ammunition. We were spotted. I lost my partner; bullets got him in an almost straight line down his back. I pushed him off the gun, moved forward a few feet with it and went back for the cases. The planes whirled, ready for another dive. I curled up, convinced they would get me this time. Some instinct concerning my manhood made me put the two metal cases across my middle parts. It was ridiculous. One bullet into either of those cans and away I'd go, balls and all. Help came; the sunken road was reached with all the guns intact, mine still bloody. Before dark they were on the job, in full blast. They bubbled over with heat, drying up. For the final burst we all urinated into a steel helmet. Some liquid was poured into each gun as the light of the day ended. We cheered. We shouted abuse. The other side was silent, strangely silent. A field kitchen appeared and fed cold boiled rice into our muddy hands. We ate, then raised them for more – and more. Our water bottles were filled. The guns drank also. Suddenly there was silence. I sat, leaning against the wall, carefully lighting a cigarette. What I dreaded most was not happening. There were no tears yet.

John Lepper wrote a poem about that day. He had survived. Parts of it still tug my memory.

> The sun warmed the valley
> But no birds sang
> The sky was rent with shrapnel
> And metallic clang
>
> * * *
>
> Men torn by shell-shards lay
> Still on the ground
> The living sought shelter
> Not to be found
>
> Holding their hot rifles
> Flushed with the fight
> Sweat-streaked survivors
> Willed for the night.

That night Bert, given charge of a small platoon of men, lost most of them through sheer panic. He left the line. John had cataracts painfully forming on both eyes. He wore a perpetual frown. Giles had colic, and went around doubled up. The next day Tom Wintringham was wounded and carried away. The running battles continued. My rifle was replaced, but Nathan, our staff officer, kept me at Battalion headquarters, less than fifty yards behind the front line. Giles was there.

We both acted as runners, Giles to the French sector, myself to the German anti-Nazi sector. We each knew the languages. I saw John. His eyes were getting worse. I told him to see Nathan, to get a note to the battalion doctor at our medical department, housed farther down the road. Every morning and evening we were heavily bombed by huge black planes. They were Italian, flying low in arrow formation. We could see the pilots. Our only cover was under some rocks. As the bombs fell, the very earth and rock lifted us up, then down. Then one glorious day, as we prepared to take cover, a few tiny Russian fighter planes whizzed up and buzzed around them. They turned back, slowly. One bomber came down in flames. We cheered; a Spanish company fired shots in the air and cried, 'Olé!'

John stayed at the hospital. I joined him. I vomited continually. We were both given notes recommending our repatriation. Nathan said he would let us go: 'One with an ulcer, the other almost blind, I don't see how you can be any further use to us here. Cheer up. You've both done your best, and I will take care of Giles. As for Bert Overton, I can promise nothing. He is in danger – from his own side.' When the truck came to take us away, Giles was sad. 'See you in London. Adios. Salud!' He was better now. Our old relationship was over.

Back in Albacete we saw the political commissar and offered to work in the rearguard. He gave us jobs in the Brigade news department. Later on he changed his mind. Every man was wanted at the front. Yes, he said, regardless of our disabilities. I then remembered a visit from a newspaper man who was in touch with friends in London. We were told then that on no account should we return to the front line: his contacts were working hard for a reasonable arrangement for all volunteers in our position. Did this commissar know about this? Was he acting under orders? I knew nothing, except that I was becoming almost paranoid concerning the Communist Party. I told John I still had some money. We decided to make our way home. In Valencia we were arrested. Having already given an account of what took place during the next three months, I will not deal with it all now, except the bare facts. Even this makes me feel sick, and I begin to itch with fleas and lice. It was a steady progress through jails, camps, then more jails. Our ailments became worse, especially John's. He wept with pain. And the visits by commissars with their questions. Were we fascists? Were we Trotskyists? – even worse in their minds. Who did we meet in Valencia? Had we underground contacts in Albacete? It seems unbelievable, but don't forget that this was after May 1937, when the communists, aided by the Civil Guard, mopped up all their critics and separatist, fellow anti-fascists. George Orwell was caught up in the midst of it in Catalonia. But John and I were small fry. What really bothered them was the people we knew – outside Spain. Then one day our cell door was opened, and our names were called. We were for release. It was a trick, surely. They would shoot us and then tell our friends we had been killed fighting at the front, like heroes.

However, our orders were to report to the political commissar. He told us to live in Albacete barracks and wait. I asked about Giles. He was at the front – Brunete this time. And Bert? Dead; killed in action. We waited for a month, and received some pay. Then a meeting was called. Comrade Harry Pollitt was going to speak to all British volunteers in Albacete. He gave a speech on morale, and was not entirely out of sympathy towards those of us awaiting repatriation. At the end of his talk he called me back. 'Don't be afraid, comrade,' he said. 'What with your family and your friends, you have been more trouble to me than the whole British Battalion put together.' He put his arm across my shoulders and handed me a letter. 'Here, read this and tell me what you think.' It was from Stephen. It told me that I only had to tell the bearer of the letter what I wanted, and he would arrange it. I replied that I wanted to go home. I was ill. Harry then said I would be on my way within a week. I asked about John Lepper. He said he was going to see about him also. 'You must, please,' I said. 'He is in great pain.' In Harry Pollitt's opinion, I was told later, I was an ordinary, decent, working class chap who had got into the hands of the kind of intellectuals the party could well do without. Well, I can't go along with that, but perhaps, over the years, the same could have been applied to Harry Pollitt.

I went to Madrigueras to get my clothing. It was all cleaned and beautifully laid out, waiting for me. Father, mother and son hugged me all at once. I gave the father my overcoat to keep him warm in the fields. We embraced. It was goodbye. In Albacete I told John I would do all I could to get him back, which I did. A fortnight after I returned to London I received a letter from Harry. Why had I not been in touch with him? After all, I was still a party member. I replied that Spain had made me into something of a pacifist. He wrote back:

Franco's cavalry advance between Vinaroz and Castellón de la Plana. Several days later they were to be driven back along the same road

Mob violence in Madrid. The scene after socialist and communist strikers had raided an opposition news office and destroyed thousands of political pamphlets

Street fighting in Madrid

Civil guards question a communist suspect in Saragossa

General Franco's infantry marches through a village as it approaches Santander, August 1937

Firing on a communist farm outside Santander

Women of Malaga give the fascist salute as they take part in a thanksgiving service in February 1937

Nationalists enter a street in Santander, ruined after the fighting, 27 August 1937

Nationalists pose for a film

Nationalist artillery battery trained on the government lines at Teruel, February 1938

A prisoner is brought in. Photograph by Robert Capa

Berjas Blancas, after the fascist occupation, January 1939

Kurski station, Moscow. A warm greeting for Spanish refugee communist youngsters, newly clad in Soviet sailor uniforms

General Yagüe and his troops kneel in prayer in the Plaza Catalunia, Barcelona, January 1939

General Franco's troops are played into Barcelona, 30 January 1939

The Condor Legion starts out on its triumphant procession through Berlin at the end of the Spanish war

'Take your time. Have a rest and you will soon get over it. Then, one day we will find a place in our ranks for you again. Fraternally yours, Harry.' I think I liked him, after all.

And now. I feel that ever since Spain I have been living with ghosts, and as I get older they become more friendly. There are people who say that writing a poem can help you to contain an emotional experience. I have written a poem, but the emotion lives on. I don't think I want to lose it. The poem is called simply 'Jarama Front'.

I tried not to see,
But heard his voice.
How brown the earth
And green the trees.
One tree was his.
He could not move.
Wounded all over,
He lay there moaning.

I hardly knew:
I tore his coat.
It was easy –
Shrapnel had helped.

But he was dying
And the blanket sagged.
'God bless you, Comrades,
He will thank you.'
That was all.
No slogan,
No clenched fist
Except in pain.

The experiences of many people leave unseen scars, on the mind, in the heart. If this is true, my scar is Spain. Along with this condition, memories, impressions, remain. Martínez, an Anarcho-Syndicalist who lay dying in an Albacete hospital and who passed his human, mutual-aid philosophy on to me. I was his only visitor, his only mourner, walking alone behind the hearse which carried his bare coffin. Once clear of the town, the driver stopped his skinny horse, and helped me

5—TDD • •

up, to ride beside him. At the burial ground I threw some wild flowers on to the coffin, before the diggers covered it with earth. Alongside the driver, we trotted back. 'A friend of yours?' he asked. 'Yes,' I said, 'a friend.' I could have added – of yours also.

The small Irish company, who held a meeting as they moved into action, elected a new leader, passed a resolution demanding their right to be kept apart from the British Battalion. Tom Wintringham, soldier and poet with infinite compassion. He blamed himself for the promotion of Bert and the tragic fiasco that followed. Giles, who years later took an overdose of pills, and was found dead in a lonely hotel room in America. John, 'seeker after truth', who died of a malignant disease in an English countryside hospital, the land he loved around him.

The solitary volunteer who walked across Spain alone. He reached Madrigueras, and asked me, 'Where's Franco?'

John H. Bassett

INTERNATIONAL BRIGADER 3

It was a moment I shall remember sharply until I die, for my mind, like a cheap camera, makes the most of the bright moments: the miseries fade. At three o'clock one morning in the early summer of 1938, I was standing with seven companions, and a shepherd, on a crest of the Pyrenees. The cold mists were beginning to rise; my nose was bleeding from my unusual exertions at such a height.

When I looked towards the north, the land was a mirror of the sky, sprinkled with the twinkling constellations of the towns and villages of a France at peace... When I turned and faced the south, the sky was as starry, but the land lay in darkness – except for the beam of a solitary searchlight, groping vainly in the sky. As I watched, there came a succession of bright flashes as the bombs rained their death. I waited, in helpless anger, but no sound came; the town was Rosas, far inside Spain.

I could still have turned back to a France which in a few wondrous weeks I had come to love – a love that has never changed – but having conquered all my fears I was impelled by an irresistible inertia. After a brief rest, I followed the last of our shepherd guides as he strode over the goat tracks with his hands behind his back, into a land torn by fratricidal strife and bitterness.

One evening about a month earlier, I had left Victoria Station with an old friend of my Cambridge days. We had caught the night boat to Ostend, bought a couple of ancient bicycles with shrivelled saddles, and pedalled south to Paris through the battlefields of Flanders. The ubiquitous monuments to the fallen only strengthened our resolution – for *that* war, organized by incompetents, had been but senseless slaughter in the mud, whereas we were on our way to fight in the sun on behalf of the working people of the world. I am sure that the Spanish sun played a great part in the formation of the International Brigades – we would have volunteered less eagerly for a struggle in the rain or snow.

We stayed in Paris for a few unforgettable weeks, living in a working class hostel in the Rue des Chaufourniers, into whose bar, with its zinc counter and scrubbed tables, came men of every colour and tongue. Overcoming the barriers of language, Swedish and Norwegian sailors, Danish students, American artists, British engineers, unemployed American negroes and Jews fleeing from Hitler put the world to rights – men from comfortable homes and refugees who had nothing to lose.

I know exactly what Hemingway meant when he called Paris 'a moveable feast'. It epitomized qualities of hope and mystery that are vanishing. Now, it is becoming difficult to dream, and we are obsessed with the dissection and measurement of everything. We visited the Eiffel Tower, Notre Dame and Sacré Coeur. We went to all the Folies, with their disturbing nude charades. I remember one cheap theatre where a beautiful stripling held us all in thrall like a Pied Piper. Many of us were obliged to visit the *maisons de tolerance*, often returning drunkenly to our bar with hilarious and exaggerated tales.

After a thorough medical examination in the Union office in the Rue Mathurin Moreau, my friend and I travelled by train to Perpignan, in the company of an American sailor, three Italians who had fled from Mussolini to Luxembourg, a Pole, a Czech and another Englishman who had been godfather to one of Harry Pollitt's children. We conversed deviously. I could speak French to the men from Luxembourg, the Pole could converse with the Czech, and the Czech was able to make sense of the Yank's peculiar Yiddish.

After a huge meal with unlimited wine, we cheerfully boarded an open truck and drove into the foothills of the Pyrenees. I can still see the huge insects flying into the headlamps, and the clenched fists of workers returning from the fields. I can still hear the incredible chorus of a million cicadas that filled the night when our engine rumbled to a stop.

I surrendered my passport, reluctantly – in those days it was a proud document, and Viscount Halifax would protect us through thick and thin. We were issued with rope-soled shoes, and followed a French shepherd on a tortuous journey that had been made illegal by the farce of 'non-intervention'. The other Englishman had been left behind. He had drunk too much in the middle of the day, and had failed to show up in the evening. We followed a succession of shepherds over the frontier into Spain, and at six in the morning we were drinking thick milky coffee in a squat stone farmhouse with a big wood fire in the middle of the room, the smoke finding its way slowly through a hole in the blackened roof. We shared the coffee with sunburned labourers and two *soldados* – the first purposefully armed men I had ever seen.

Refreshed, we made our way down through the cork oaks into the valley. The journey was painful, for our insteps had become very bruised through the pliant soles of the *alpargatas*. We rested again when we reached the road, but were too excited to sleep; an hour later a *camión* arrived and drove us to a monastery on the outskirts of Figueras. We were welcomed by a slogan over the arch: *Resistir es Vencer*, 'to resist is to conquer', and as we drove into the dusty square we laughed at the sight of a sentry sitting with his leg over the arm of an old leather chair. We had clearly come to join a people's army.

At Figueras we lived in a civilized manner. There was a variety of good food and drink, and we were waited upon. We slept in beds and were issued with soap and towels. The library had been emptied of its religious content and filled with political books and tracts in every language, with the orange covers of Gollancz very much in evidence. There was even a radio set, full of static and catchy Spanish *pasos dobles*.

After another medical examination, this time very cursory, we signed on for the duration. Some of the recruits were persuaded to join the *Partido Communista España*, but I considered this step to be unwise, for victory was far from being in the bag. We were issued with thin tunics and trousers. Mine came halfway up my legs, but an old seamstress did her best with them. Every evening, Captain Ollerenshaw would open a small bar for about half an hour, and we acquired a taste for Spanish vermouth and soda. He tried to sell me a pair of army boots with very square toes; later, I wished I had bought them. At night, the power from Barcelona was often cut off, and we would stand in darkness on the flat roofs and watch the flash of distant bombs, like summer lightning in the sierras.

In the cool of the morning we learned to drill to Spanish commands. No ammunition was available, so we shot 'dry', squinting along an old rifle mounted on a wooden box while shouting instructions to a man holding a wooden bull's eye on a stick. Whenever we broke off, we picked figs, almonds, pomegranates and unripe oranges, and squirted wine or water from the skinbags. We threw stones at scorpions and other strange creatures. In the heat of the day we swam in the stone pool where the old women washed the clothes, and at dusk we paraded in the square while the flag of the Republic was lowered to the sound of a bugle. The war was still a long way off, and it was all rather fun.

One morning, two weeks later, we were aroused at dawn, given a loaf and a tin of sardines, and taken south in an open *camión* to Barcelona. Pausing briefly in the Ramblas while the driver visited a whorehouse, we drove on south through endless vistas of olive groves and vineyards and trees hanging with the brown locust beans I had eaten as a child and which kept all constipation at bay. I had no need of locust in Spain – on the contrary. We came at last to Montblanch, a small town huddling in deep blue shadows around the church at the foot of a great hill. We drove over the bridge to be welcomed at another monastery by the sign: *Brigadas Internacionales: Centro de Recepción.*

Suddenly, the war became very close. It was a time for truth. Not only was there the constant rumbling reminder from beyond the Ebro, but all the decencies of life had vanished. I had to adapt myself, very rapidly, to living like an animal. I slept on a strawbag crawling with lice. I ate and drank from one tin dish that I had been forced to 'organize' – a euphemism for theft that had been coined by the battalion. The food was tasteless and monotonous – dry bread, lentils, chickpeas (*garbanzos*) and small shrivelled fish with glazed eyes, cooked in oil drums. We queued for this diet in the open, in the company of a great bitch with raw teats who waited for what we threw away – not in satiety but in disgust. The 'coffee' was said to be charred barley or corn. There was never any milk or sugar, and it was the sugar that we began to miss above all else.

Montblanch was also the Catalonian centre through which the sick and wounded were returned to the front when considered fit. They were tough, and very cynical and scarred by bullets, shrapnel and lanced boils. All their idealism had gone. One day, I was waiting in the queue for *comida* when a stranger came along, crying: 'I hear there's somebody just out from London!' Smiling, I gave him the clenched fist salute. He simply called me a bloody idiot, and moved on without another word.

One afternoon, at the time of the siesta, we were digesting our *garbanzos* when a sleek Spanish captain, in a Sam Browne and polished boots, summoned us to an *hora political*. Nobody was interested, and after an argument he forced us downstairs at the point of his gun. We sat sullenly in the shade of some olive trees while a Spanish commissar read an article from the *Frente Rojo*, a badly printed paper that was always pretending that the Republic was winning on all fronts, even when retreating. After the interpreter had made translations in four or five languages, questions were invited. The British gave one concerted roar: '*When are we going home?*' The next question came from a Canadian who demanded a pair of socks.

I had come too late. All the romance had gone. It might have been different had there been a prospect of victory. But there was no escape, and I tried to make the best of things. I steadily acquired more Spanish, including the oaths with which the Spaniards defecated on everything, especially the symbols of the Church – even befouling the twenty-four balls of the twelve apostles. Our spirits would rise at night when we went into the town to drink huge bottles of *vino rojo* with great dishes of seasoned tomatoes and onions, for which we would exchange some of our precious tobacco. I had retained a few Gauloises, and slept with them inside my shirt. I never once saw food in any Spanish shop, and *quieres cambiar*? (do you want to swap?) enabled us to get some of the nutrients for which our bodies craved.

One evening, we were sitting along the kerb of the main street, waiting for the cinema to open with a dubbed film of Loretta Young. The men began to sing, in every language. The British sang, 'There's a Valley in Spain called Jarama', and 'No Pasarán', and 'We came to sunny Spain, to make the people smile again, and to chase the fascist bastards over hill and over plain'.

One tune, in Spanish, everybody sang. When the polyglot army sang 'The Crossing of the Ebro', with its plaintive: '*Y Manuelo . . . y Manuelo . . .*' the shivers ran up and down my spine and I knew that I had found a small place in history. Had *vanity* brought us there, to be among the few, with the eyes of the world on us? We may, in retrospect, have been misguided, but never again will men of every creed and tongue go to war with the ideals with which the volunteers went to Spain. It was indeed a time of hope, when a man with a rifle had some power to divert the tide of human affairs. Now, we drift at the mercy of events too vast and complex to be managed. Men will never go to war like that again, for war will never be as simple. Now except where information is controlled, we all know too much, and our wills are sapped – and therein lies the danger to democracy.

One night, a group of us were summoned to the front. The newcomers were relieved, for the waiting had become intolerable. Despite assurances that everything would be provided at the front, a veteran advised us to take what we could. We rolled our blankets around our bodies, concealing them under our tunics, and mounted the *camión* like Michelin men. The ride over the mountains in the cold darkness was a nightmare, but at last we dropped down to the pontoons that had been strung across the Ebro, and climbed up through the ruins of Mora del Ebro towards the front. The moon had now risen, and by its light half a dozen of us found our way to the British contingent, through the strange hiss of tired bullets and the stench of distended mules. Nobody was awake to welcome us. I rolled up in my blanket on the open ground and tried to sleep. It was very cold.

The next morning I was asked for my next of kin, and given a shovel and an old rifle with a loose stock. The bullets had to be carried in my pockets, and the weight of four grenades pulled my belt down over my buttocks.

My company was then in immediate reserve. From the grove, where we were dispersed among the olives, I could see the ridge along which ran our forward trenches. With the first good light, a spotting plane droned overhead, while everybody caught in the open stayed motionless. An hour later, the shells began to blast the ridge, and I was near enough to see the bright red wounds of men being carried down the hill. The shells came every day, and would be followed by the Savoias and Junkers, so clear in the eternal sun that I could have counted the rivets on their metal skins. I had been advised to dig a trench for myself, wherever I might stop for more than an hour. I soon learned that it was every man for himself; once, when bombs began to fall in the grove, I was diving into my hole when I found it occupied by my company commander.

At night, we were sent to the front to dig trenches while the day shift slept. The skies were always clear, and even the stars gave us enough light. There was little comradeship; hope and curiosity had gone. Everybody seemed tired, tense, and intent only on survival. The men's biggest fears seemed to be of the foul practices of the Moors.

Our weapons were pitiful; I am sure that if Hitler had wished the Republic could have been defeated much sooner. Our company had 'mexikanski' rifles, and two clumsy Tokarov and Dikatrov machine-guns, always jamming with sand. Occasionally, we saw a few tubby little Moscas – a Russian copy of an American fighter – and a few tanks with three-inch guns. It has now become clear that the war was a trial of weapons and tactics, the forerunner of wars in Korea, Vietnam and Israel. In 1936 the Russians were using a form of radar in the defence of Madrid; the Condor Legion had all the practice in the world, with little opposition; and towards the end of the struggle Juan Negrín admitted that he had been negotiating for weapons even from Germany.

After I had spent a few days in the grove, our front was broken and we were ordered up. As we neared the fighting, we became afraid, and were bunched together, before being reluctantly dispersed by our commander. The hill we tried to retake had been terraced for vines, and we scrambled up from ledge to ledge, helped only by the gun of a solitary tank on the road at the foot of the hill, and the cries of our commissar, screaming 'death to the fascist bastards!' Halfway up, we were forced to stop, crouching behind a dry stone terrace with the bullets singing over our heads. I looked back, when there was a lull: the hillside was littered with blankets, picks, shovels and grenades; we had jettisoned everything for mobility.

Under the burning sun, we clung to that hill all day, strafed from time to time by Messerschmitt 109s. Our rifles were often too hot to handle, and we ran out of ammunition. I was sent back down the hill, passing the first dead men I had ever seen. A pile of rope-handled boxes had been thrown out of the tank, and lay under the barrel of the gun. As I stooped to grab a box, the gun went off. The blast nearly knocked me silly and my ears sang for days. I have always believed that it was the stupidity of the Spanish gunner that caused me to go deaf before I was forty. When I got back to my comrades I was at once cursed for bringing up a case with the wrong markings, and had to go back for another.

We were moved at night from one part of the front to another. I never saw a map, and nothing was ever explained to me. We always followed somebody who understood Spanish and who seemed to have an inkling of what we were doing. Food found its way to us at dusk, usually soup with potato and the meat of *burro* (donkey), that could be chewed for hours. I always felt quite brave after the soup, and I was sure that it had been laced with cognac, of which our commander always had a good supply. It was a very powerful spirit; it would ignite readily with a spark from our wick *mecheros* (lighters). During the hot days in the trenches we had nothing but sardines and stale bread – no water or wine, for we had nothing to keep them in.

One day during those weeks at the front, the accuracy of the shelling turned my stomach to water. As the guns modified their range, the warning rush of air became shorter and shorter, the bursts closer and closer, until dirt and stones poured into the trench and rattled on the shovel which I was holding over my head and neck. As the apprentice, I had been allotted the end of the line, adjoining a narrow macadam road along which I expected to see enemy vehicles at any minute. All day, men would crawl over me and relieve themselves at the end of the trench. I ceased to bother to brush the flies off my face. I dreamed of tea in my mother's garden in suburbia, of pints of mild and bitter in oak-beamed pubs, and I could not help wishing that I had never come.

During the night, our sleep was fitful. We took turns to prowl in no man's land, alert for every sound, among the shattered trees and the yellow picric of shells that had split and failed to explode. Almost every night somebody would take fright, and for five or ten minutes whole hillsides would be lit up, to a cacophony of rifle fire and bursting grenades.

We were withdrawn after about three weeks of the most unpleasant time of my life. We sat around all day in an olive grove, while the commander and his commissar consumed cognac. I was given every tedious chore. One day I was sent out with two others to round up some deserters. Later, I was to feel ashamed: I had never seen men so utterly dispirited, yet I had put a bullet in the breech and cocked the pin of my rifle, and was ready to kill them.

About a week later, when we were expecting to be sent up again, I was summoned to the *estado mayor*, in a dugout in the hillside. I was told that because of my experience in the British Post Office, a fact which I had disclosed earlier, I was being transferred to the *Brigada Transmisiones*. I was very relieved, but when I returned to my comrades they all thought I was forsaking the frying pan for the fire. In fact, the transfer probably saved my life.

I spent the rest of my war with the *transmisiones*. At night, I would clamber for miles over the hills, with a heavy reel of wire on a metal bracket strapped to my back. The bar, through the thin tunic, made my back raw. I was again the monkey, and after struggling for miles with a full reel was always the last to be spliced to the wire that had been laid. When we reached roads, we had to climb trees from which to string the wire across above the traffic. The days never brought rest, as I had hoped. Shells, bombs and wandering tanks had a knack of breaking our wires, and we were out all day repairing them, dodging the bombs and shells. I spliced many wires that moments before had passed intact through my hand. I worked very fast. Oddly enough, I had been prompted to take out a pair of side-cutters, a tool with which I was very familiar and which proved invaluable. When at sundown we returned to base, the cold greasy *garbanzos* would be almost uneatable.

The routine was the same, day after day, and I lost track of time. The nights lengthened slowly, and then came the last action of the British in the Sierra Pandols, where my old company was decimated. I only saw one or two of the men again, and they had run away. They were hardly to be blamed, for Juan Negrín had announced his intention of withdrawing the volunteers.

Negrín was one of the few leaders to come out of the war without recrimination, dying in Mexico with dignity. Those, like the peasant commander El Campesino, and the propagandist La Pasionaria, who had exhorted us to die fighting rather than live forever on our knees, found their comfortable ways to Moscow. Throughout the war, the communist parties of the world moved their favoured men in and out of Spain at will; but had it not been for Negrín's gesture, the rank and file of the volunteers would have been forsaken.

I can recall, with pride, that as I recrossed the Ebro I felt sad that my war had been so short. I had not relished the life in the trenches, but I could have endured the *transmisiones* as long as health permitted, and some hope of victory remained – or even stalemate.

We were moved from place to place, from old houses to desecrated churches whose aisles resounded to the incessant popping of champagne corks – at ten pesetas each bottle was a day's pay, but there was nothing else to buy. At one *hacienda* near Marsa, thousands of English books had been collected, and we read and argued all day long. The power to the house had been disrupted, but we stripped some wire from a bombed factory and hooked the house wiring to the overhead cables, and then read far into the night. It was a strange, argumentative army of thinkers.

One night, of all nights, they chose to move us during a raging thunderstorm. We struggled along flooded roads, lit up by lightning, to the railway station, with water often up to our waists. Hours later, after drying out and being fed in Barcelona, we entrained for Ripoll, where after a false start, far too comfortable to last, we were quartered in the theatre. It was a dark, filthy place; sometimes men would shake their lice-ridden blankets out over the balcony, to howls of rage from the stalls.

I now became very weak and yellow with jaundice, and had to find my own way to a military hospital at Vich, about twenty miles to the south. A peasant on the train gave me a boiled egg. At Vich, I spent two weeks, in a bed, with much better food and unlimited tobacco. Then, on hearing that the British were on the point of leaving Spain, I slipped through the guards with authority from the doctor to visit *el dentista.* Alas, when I reached Ripoll the rumour had been false, and I regretted having left hospital. I was still very weak, and was unable to go to Barcelona for the farewell parade of the Brigades.

The British authorities found every excuse to delay our return, even compelling us to be vaccinated. But at last, in December, we took the train to La Tour de Carol, sent off by a small band playing the Republican anthem – the *Himno de Riego* – a tune that still brings tears for what might have been.

In France, we were given a huge meal, and some went back to queue for another. Afterwards, so strong was the desire for sugar, some of the men bought milk chocolate and dipped it in sweetened condensed milk. It was all too much, too strange and too sudden.

The train was obliged to bypass Paris, for fear of demonstrations.

We stopped once, and were greeted by the Salvation Army, with trolleys of sweet milky coffee and warm French bread. We were about to gorge ourselves when Sam Wild, our battalion commander, cried out: 'Everybody back on the train! We're not going to accept charity!' Like sheep we went back, and I can still see those puzzled faces on the platform. I have since thought deeply about the meaning of words, and their power. We had crossed mountains to fight 'fascism', suffered indignities because of the imperative of our 'political duty', and behaved like sheep at the cry of 'charity'. I now know that charity is the hallmark of the true religion, the truth whose well is within us all. Our Spanish dreams had been made of words not strong enough to withstand reality.

We crossed from Dieppe. The lavatories were soon ankle-deep in vomit. At Victoria Station we were welcomed by Clem Attlee, who had given his name to a company of the British Battalion. We marched through the streets to the plaudits of millions, it seemed. We were all very proud, and everything now seemed to have been worth while, for we were home, and alive. A few days later, I was given a Co-op suit. The adventure was over.

The years have passed, and I know that I have changed with them. But events and disclosures have often given me cause to wonder if our struggle had been any less futile than that of Flanders, if we had only given Hitler a little more time to practise, if we had only been struggling to replace one tyranny by another. Had Buenavertura Durruti, the anarchist, been the wisest of all who had fought in Spain for liberty?

III

Journal of a Naive Revolutionary

PHILIP TOYNBEE

Journal of a Naive Revolutionary

When we look back on a distant period of our own lives we seem to be faced with two quite contrary temptations. The more obvious (but perhaps for that reason the less insidious) is the temptation to be over-indulgent, to sentimentalize the charms of our youth, even to regret that we have now become, in contrast to those days of hope, so crabbed and cribbed, so set in the dull habits of maturity. The opposite temptation urges us to mock and despise the silliness of long ago, with the implied assumption that we are now *very far* from silly; that we have long put behind us all such childish things and attained a cool objectivity which enables us to look back on our past selves with admirable detachment.

When, for my present purposes, I first re-read the journal which I kept during my visit to Republican Spain over Christmas 1936 I confess that I nearly succumbed to the second of these temptations without much of a struggle. How *could* I – *I* – ever have thought or felt, still less solemnly written, such simple-minded and indoctrinated rubbish! But after thinking harder about that time and this time I began to recognize an undeniable continuity between the man of twenty and the man of sixty. My beliefs have radically changed during the intervening forty years; I have learned to express myself at least with greater caution, and surely with a more practised skill as well. I am amazed, in my present state of advanced middle age, by the boundless and bounding energy of that young 'student delegate' making his breathless pilgrimage to the contemporary Mecca of his revolutionary faith. But though I hope and believe that I now know a great deal more than I knew then, I doubt whether the congenital naivety of this particular young man is of a kind which can be uprooted by a mere forty years of living.

In fact I respond to these passages from my ancient diary with something more than a hot flush of shame. I respond, at moments, with a vibrant sympathy, curiously intermingled with a rueful act of 'recognition', in the strict sense of 'recognizing' the *de facto* reality of that faraway young man, of recognizing that he was indeed myself, and that I am he.

But there is no reason on earth why this admission of a continuous identity should preclude a proper severity, any more than we should ever look with over-indulgent eyes at our *present* selves. Stand *there*! Admit the identification. But then stand back; turn round and look at what you are or what you were with the coldest eye you can contrive. The result will not be the objective portrait of a human being, since no such thing has ever been painted or written by anyone. But at least it should be a little closer to the mysterious 'truth' than if no conscious effort had been made to avoid the twin temptations of over-indulgence and sneering disassociation.

But before I begin the attempt to re-create that short and distant period of my own past it seems that I ought to justify the enterprise if I can; that I must find some more or less persuasive reason why anyone in 1976, almost certainly harassed by a great number of immediate and utterly different preoccupations, should wish to consider the curious ways of a young upper middle class Englishman in 1936.

This is not the place for a historical judgement on the Spanish Civil War: I leave that in the infinitely more capable hands of Hugh Thomas, Claud Cockburn and Brian Crozier. And if that young visitor to Spain had represented no more than himself he might have the right to be resurrected as an outlandish idiosyncracy, but that right could have been won only by the artful method of his resurrection. I mean that everything, in that case, would have depended on my own skill as a resurrectionist; on my almost huckster-like ability to persuade the passers-by into my own tent. But if, as I do indeed believe, the Philip Toynbee of Christmas 1936 was truly typical of one section of a generation, then I can justify his resurrection on the safer ground that his journal is a historical document of at least minor and peripheral significance. To read this document is to read (no doubt in an extreme, perhaps in an almost preposterous, form) the kind of diary which many young men and women might have written at the time, whether in Western Europe or in the United States, in Australia or even in the universities of India.

If I were to claim that this figure is an adequate and complete representative I'm sure his surviving comrades would immediately set up a loud and angry baying of denial and disassociation. Perhaps they would be justified in doing so. But this young man is, after all, the only one I've got. He will have to do. I think he *will* do as a means of re-creating at least one element in a historical epoch which now seems very historical indeed.

I had joined the Communist Party of Great Britain (Student Section) in November 1935, during my first term at Oxford. It is sometimes supposed by those who look back on that period without having known it that this was an almost obligatory initiation for every new student, and particularly for an ex-public school Oxbridge student, at that particular exotic period of university history. In fact during the whole of my three years at Oxford there were never more than 200 Communist Party members in a university of more than 3,500, and this high peak was reached only for a single term in 1937. At least half this membership consisted of ex-grammar school boys, and there wasn't, so far as I can remember, a single Old Etonian among us. The *open* communists, alongside whom I was soon to be rather prominently exposed, were never more than thirty or forty. More significant still, there was never a time during the thirties when the membership of the Oxford University Labour Club was as high as that of the Conservative Association.

And, as in every period in every English university, the great majority of students were scarcely interested in politics at all; they were far more preoccupied with doing well in their studies, with playing competitive games, with literary clubs and dramatic societies, choirs and orchestras, with friendships, with food, drink and sex. So the fact that I joined the Communist Party so readily and so quickly needs some sort of explanation. It is bound to be an uncertain one, for I probably understand the muddle of my motives only a little better now than I did then. Revolt against parental and school authority? Of course. The pleasures and inner security provided by belonging to a semi-secret society? Not a doubt of it. The pure romanticism of red flags and clenched fists? Who could deny it.

But there were other and weightier motives as well. It was not unnatural that a young man who looked about him in 1935, and who had spent three months of that year in Nazi Germany, should have learned to fear and detest fascism. It was not unnatural that the Communist Party should have seemed the most effective instrument in the necessary struggle to unite all anti-fascists in a common front. Besides, this was a period of deep depression in the British economy; of devastating unemployment and scandalous malnutrition, accompanied by gross affluence for the few, and cushioned comfort for nearly all the professional middle classes. (My father, a 'poor professor', employed two maids, a cook and a gardener; he owned one large house in Yorkshire and another in London.) The Communist Party of Great Britain could easily justify its claim to be in the vanguard of the fight against a monstrous 'National' government which cared little or nothing for poverty at home and almost as little for the present reality and future international dangers of fascism in Europe.

I note, at this point, that my words begin to reverberate with ancient echoes; they begin to sound like a passage from one of the hundred or so speeches which I must have made during those appalling prewar years. And even as the old words come tumbling back into my mind and on to the keys of my typewriter I feel the definite stirring of an old anger. A legitimate anger; indeed an *obligatory* anger, so I still believe, against a despicable government and a rotten ruling class.

It now seems very odd that some of us should have chosen, in our righteous anger, to give our slavish support to an even more horrible government and our allegiance to a party which, whenever it has achieved power, has made Mr Neville Chamberlain look like an angel of sensitive and intelligent goodwill. Well, in our hunger for an earthly paradise we grossly deceived ourselves about Stalin's Russia and foolishly accepted the harsh and cynical methods of our own party. I can find no effective excuse for this wilful blindness; but nor have I ever felt particularly tempted to beat my breast about the wickedness of my former ways. (The chest has to be puffed out a long way before the breast can be beaten to full effect.)

I read the news of the right-wing military rising against the

Republican government of Spain on 19 July 1936, and in the London bedsitter of my close friend Esmond Romilly. In a book which I wrote nearly twenty years later about Esmond and another friend, both of whom were killed in the Second World War, I recorded the event like this: 'Over our hurried breakfast we read the news of the "Generals' Revolt" against the Spanish government. I myself – and it is a sign of my political innocence, even of my frivolity – was excited and pleased by the revolt, believing that it must be quickly crushed and that its suppression would be a heavy blow against reaction everywhere. Esmond – it was a sign of his growing political seriousness – was alarmed and apprehensive.' This still seems to be a fair enough description both of myself and of my friend.

The Spanish Civil War lasted two years and eight months, and during nearly the whole of that period I was passionately, actively but only distantly involved in that dreadful and agonizing conflict. In that same *Memoir of the 'Thirties* from which I have already quoted I described myself as 'proliferating Spanish Defence Committees throughout the university as a moth lays its eggs in a clothes cupboard'. I was also making speeches all over the place; organizing meetings; helping to launch press campaigns . . . The main objects of all these frenzied activities were to collect money and food for the Spanish government and to oppose our own government's strictly observed posture of non-intervention on the grounds – fair enough grounds – that this international policy was being contemptuously disregarded by Italy and Germany, and was therefore a major cause of Franco's continuing successes.

The great majority of English men and women who gave any thought to the matter were supporters of the Spanish Republic, either because they believed – quite mistakenly – that it was a liberal-democratic regime on the English model; or because they knew it was not and hoped for a communist revolution in Spain; or simply because they calculated that a Republican victory would be more to this country's national advantage than the victory of a fascist general who was already in close alliance with Hitler and Mussolini. Only a *very* few people in England actively spoke or campaigned for Franco; so it would be wrong to think of these years as powerfully divisive in this country, setting fathers against sons and sons against mothers, in the way that the months of the Munich agreement and the Suez adventure were actively and painfully divisive.

However, my own mother's attitude was ambiguous in the extreme: a recent convert to the Roman Catholic Church she had also moved a long way to the Right since her (incredible!) membership of the Labour Party during my early childhood. Behind a transparent smokescreen of 'a plague on both your houses' her preference for the House of Franco was seldom very carefully disguised. This exacerbated a family conflict which was already waspish enough; and hard words were all too often exchanged during my holidays from Oxford.

So if I concentrate here on a short period at an early stage of the war this is not because it tells the whole story of my own eager if bumbling 'relationship' with the Spanish Civil War, but because it provides a sharp and concise definition of an attitude which was common to a great many of us at that time. I have made these selections from my diary solely on the criterion of typicality. I hope I shall not forget that the comments which follow the quotations will be every bit as typical of certain elderly Englishmen in 1976 as the diary itself was typical of certain young English students in 1936. No doubt both the diary and my present commentary on it will seem equally of their period, equally dated, to any reader who may stumble on this combination in the year 2006.

December 22nd, 1936. (Written on the train; Port-Bou to Barcelona.) On Sunday we had our Meeting of Action in Paris – what we could all do next. I became president of it, somehow or other, and concluded the proceedings with great skill in French and English. Afterwards I was congratulated all round by the Paris group of international comrades; and how nice it is, this all-too-rare approbation of my Party. Later we had a fraction meeting [Note: Communist term for the Party's policy-making intrigues before any larger meeting with non-communists. P.T.] and it was decided that I should lead the non-party student delegation. In fact honours are being showered on my head; and I can't pretend that I dislike it . . .

On Monday we went along to the *Cité Paradis* where the whole delegation met – three French (one Tunisian); two Czechs and six of us. I was duly made leader of the delegation and went off to the Spanish Embassy to get a collective pass for all of us . . .

It was lovely weather and the Catalan coast was absolutely beautiful; red earth and rock, scattered with olives and cypresses. Later the sun went down – dark, dark red over an angular line of hills. It was all most lovely and I felt more moved than I have for a long time. Travelling into the heart of this country where *our* people are fighting for *our* things was a very stirring experience.

After lunch I and several of the other delegates talked to a POUM [Note: a non-communist radical left organization. P.T.] militiaman in the train corridor. He was charming and made me aware that even Trotskyists could be nice in this country. We all argued against him. He had fought at Huesca and was now going to do service on the coast. He assured us that this coast is very well defended and that an attack on Barcelona would be quite impossible.

December 23rd. We were at Barcelona by 6.30 and conducted to a cheap (4 pesetas – about 6d each!) restaurant by our 'copain espagnol'. Fine big meal – so not much of a food shortage! And another encouraging thing was the militiaman handing us out cartridges as keepsakes: not much of an ammunition shortage either!

Gil Martinez (my French and, of course, C.P. second-in-command) and I went to the post-office with the militiaman. The streets were full of these sweet slovenly uniforms and the buses and trams had U.G.T. and C.N.T. written on them: so had the trains. (Note: Communist and anarchist trade union organizations respectively. P.T.) The place was full of a sort of carnival atmosphere – *en pleine révolution.*

This is a workers' city at war, fighting to keep its trams and cinemas and industries in the workers' hands. Air-raid refuges were everywhere marked up; all the lights were painted blue and the windows reinforced with sticky paper to prevent them splintering.

By the G.P.O. was a boy scout's tent in the middle of the square. They were taking parcels free to worker-soldiers, and Gil gave them one for a friend of his on the Madrid front. I felt so wildly excited and yet so wretched at being a 'student delegate'. A french anarchist militiaman asked us which front we were going to, and it was bloody to have to say, to Valencia and Madrid, just to look around.

I think it will be an act of heroism if I *do* decide to obey Party instructions and go home. But I don't *know*! It's easy to think that one would fight if only one could; but would one really? In *this* mood I would, but not in all my moods.

Anyway how intoxicating to be in a city which is ours and seeing uniforms in which one can delight. Almost everywhere else I've been – possibly not Popular Front Paris – a uniform has meant an enemy . . .

On the train to Valencia boys threw oranges to us as we steamed out of each little station, and all the way along the line the smiling people outside clenched their fists as we passed, and we saluted back. There were no separate classes; the ticket-collector decided who would go in which compartments. This sort of thing makes one feel that the bourgeoisie has already vanished.

Very tired and late into Valencia. Gil and I left the others and went off in search of the Frente de la Juventud. The streets were full of posters and flags, and all the private cars had been commandeered by some working-class organization or other. There were armed workers outside the bigger buildings and a demonstration by a militia band collecting money for orphaned children.

Eventually we found the Frente, where we were able to explain ourselves to a French P.M. [Note: Party Member, not Prime Minister. P.T.] He too had fought at Huesca, and had been wounded in the knee. He chiefly told us about the difficulty of working with the anarchists, but how the United Socialists, which includes the Party, were steadily gaining at anarchist expense. There was a splendid air of efficiency about this place . . .

After lunch we all went in flag-draped taxis to the Students' Union. No men there at all, but lots of girls sewing flags and clothes; such sweet girls, all about 17 or 18 so far as I could tell. They pinned badges on us, produced cakes, sherry, brandy and vermouth, and soon we were in the middle of a delightful party, each of us surrounded by about four of these girls and enjoying himself enormously. They wrote messages of greeting for us to take back to students at home, and we kept on shouting 'Viva La République!' 'Viva le Peuple Espagnol!'

But we were torn away, certainly to my regret, in order to visit a militia barracks. Through tiny winding streets, holding clenched fists out of the window and the girls shouting their shrill good-byes behind us. The barracks had been a convent, converted a few months before, when the nuns had all been sent back to their homes – *not*, we were assured, molested . . .

The militiamen were so universally nice and the whole atmosphere of easy friendliness was quite delightful. For a moment, looking up at the moon, I thought of the nuns and that to many people this place would now seem positively sacrilegious. But I felt it such an unqualified blessing that these smiling worker-soldiers were there instead of the cold, stately ladies with their hoods and rosaries . . .

To various government offices and ministries: absolutely no formality anywhere . . .

Met an English journalist who had been fighting with Esmond [Note: My friend had joined the International Column, as it then was, in August or September. P.T.] and was full of affection and admiration for him. At least Es was alive a week ago. Scott Watson also told us about the murder of Party leaders by anarchists . . .

My chief impression so far is one of extraordinary lightheartedness and yet of things running remarkably smoothly as well. Two separate things are going on; the war and the revolution: not many people abroad are aware of this . . .

Christmas Eve. Once on the main Madrid road there was surprisingly little traffic; cars with CONTROL on the wind-screen, a few big lorries and quite a lot of peasant waggons. It was a lovely afternoon, and the country lovely too, red rocks almost luminous in the sunlight. We climbed a high pass, perilously, and a little later the sun went down. We sang revolutionary songs, mostly french, and drove romantically through the red-slashed sky towards Madrid . . .

At this village little boys clustered round the bus; I seized hold of one and was photographed holding him in my arms with my fist clenched above his head. There was a Party H.Q. here, as in every village. If the P has a real hold on the countryside it will indeed be a blessing. Anarchism there could be so utterly unconstructive – expropriate the landowners and then, presumably, leave the peasants as uneducated as they are today.

Perez, our Spanish (Party) guide was splendid, arranging everything with great effect and eventually even getting us some petrol. By that time it was late and very cold; I had drunk a lot and I made a little speech to the delegation, serious but also raising a laugh or two . . .

Christmas Day. Up at five and an ice-cold wash and shave. Off again in the pitch darkness of this high plateau... Some of the militia in this town were boys of about 14... A little platoon of machine-gunners... A poster announcing that the C.N.T. demands power – which shows, as I'd thought, that they haven't got much of it in the country regions...

The local mayor, a left-wing Socialist, told us that when the war started people had envisaged it simply as a defence of the liberal Republic; but later it became clear that sweeping social reforms would follow, and now almost everyone recognises that a military victory will mean 'Les Soviets Par-tout!' (All our talk about 'defence of the constitutionally-elected government of Spain' seems pretty silly out here.)

Again an account of the amazing gains made by the C.P. since the outbreak of the war... The mayor said that Madrid *cannot* fall: the defences are so perfect that it would need a major battle to win every house...

Quite suddenly we could see the whole of Madrid lying in front of us, with a slight haze hanging over it. There was white smoke rising from one or two places but not a sign of war. We were soon in the streets, and the first thing we noticed was the barricades everywhere, sand-bags and stone, beautifully constructed. A gutted church, all the windows reinforced, and houses here and there with whole walls missing... At the H.Q. of the Frente here – an old palace, very, very cold – there were pictures of Stalin on the walls and also photographs of members of the Juventud who had been killed...

Interviewed Don José Miaja, president of the delegated Junta, commander-in-chief for the defence of Madrid. He said that he is a Catholic Republican but the thing he is most proud of is that he is the general of the people. I liked him a lot...

There was a lovely girl at the Juventud, rather like Jessie Matthews, but small and plump, wearing great wide blue trousers. She could speak, alas, nothing but Spanish, yet we somehow managed to understand each other... Splendid people and I felt utterly happy talking to them all – Germans, Italians and Frenchmen as well as Spaniards – but I'm afraid much of my time was spent making eyes at Josefina Lopez! We drank rough red wine, ate hard bread and cheese... Gil and I made speeches to which one of the Spaniards made a translated reply. Then they all began singing, revolutionary songs in one language after another. Such charming people and the music, with guitars, so very moving... The Spaniards sang a new song about the barbaric bombardment of the Prado... Then the girl sang solos; a lovely voice, harsh and vibrant in the Arab manner. I sang *The Cloth-Makers' Union*; *Allelujah, I'm a Bum* and a few others... 'Mañana aqui?' I asked her when we left; and she; 'Si! Du aqui mañana?' '*Si!*' said I with the utmost enthusiasm...

No lights anywhere, not even in the Puerto. Very exhausted to bed...

Boxing Day. We got some black coffee and bread for breakfast, then packed into old cars and went out to a north-western working-class district, Tetua Las Victorias. Here quantities of little houses had been bombed to pieces: the bull-ring too. We went up on to a bit of waste land where several months ago fascist aeroplanes had machine-gunned a crowd and left the place thick with corpses. Until now I had never really *felt* about this bombing and shelling of an open city, but seeing this destruction all round me I was suddenly furious at the wantonness of it. It can serve no military purpose whatever, especially as the civilian population has utterly refused to be terrorized. And how can Franco, even in his maddest moments, suppose that he'll be able to govern a people whom he's shelled to pieces!

To a military hospital after that... It was very grim, for all its cleanliness and efficiency. I'd never envisaged the wounded, only the dead, and in some ways the wounded are more terrifying... one had lost his foot and there was another with his face horribly pushed up to one side... Mostly we spoke to the International Column people and I was deeply impressed by their smiling faces and their amazing courage. I suppose there's nowhere in the world a more admirable group of men than these gallant 15,000...

French comrades in these reserve trenches, and as we drove past them always 'Salut les copains!' and the grinning faces of the Parisian poor... Rifle-shots very close... walked into the second line, a sunken lane with sandbags covering one side, soldiers in steel helmets sitting by fires at the mouths of dug-outs, just like the War. 'Salut! Salut!' all the way along and fists hardly having time to unclench... it was darkening by now and a long red sunset silhouetted a barbed-wire entanglement... I felt absurdly miserable and moved, wishing terribly that I could stay there and fight with all these brave and smiling comrades, yet knowing that this is a stupid and childish wish and that actually I had a far harder and more heartbreaking task ahead of me than they had ... Two Soviet lorries passed us on their way up to the front, and were pointed out to us with glee. I felt gleeful too ...

Back at the Juventud Josefina was staring at me, and I felt wildly excited about her ... We played chess in the cold salon and I was easily beaten, but since I was white and she was red we took this to mean that Madrid would never fall ...

Gil, one of the Czechs and I went off to the H.Q. of the International Column. General Kleber was there and we lunched with him and his general staff. What a splendid staff, all in different uniforms or none, and united only in having hammers-and-sickles or soviet stars sewn on their tunics. And the servant girls were obviously on terms of complete equality with all these big-wigs. (Most were Spaniards, oddly enough.) I *did* like and admire them so much, and Kleber in particular. He is a big, grey-haired man with Russian eyes, one of the most impressive people I've ever met, quiet and modest yet obviously immensely capable. He talked German perfectly, English well, French and Spanish badly. He told me that John Cornford, Esmond and the rest of the ones I know were behind the lines now, after a long front-line spell. He was quite optimistic, and I felt that in this case optimism was really worth something. (Of course the frankness with which he spoke to us was mainly because he knew that we too were in the Party.) [Note: Emilio Kléber, real name Lazar Stern, a naturalized Russian of Hungarian birth, had been a communist soldier of fortune for much of his life. He disappeared in Russia during the later purges. P.T.]

K provided us with a car and we were driven up to the front line over rolling down-land. An extremely quiet sector, where a Spanish colonel asked us rather gruffly whether we were members of the 'Partido Communista'. I showed him my party card (being, I suppose, the only open member on the delegation, although I now find that there are 8 p.m.s in an 'all party' delegation of 11!) and we were taken from the H.Q. by car right up to the front line ...

The fascists were a long way off here and one could safely walk about in the open: occasionally they threw a few shells over, but ¾ of them were duds. There was a nice little Spaniard in command of mostly French troops, and I was delighted to see that he was treated just like anybody else; was indistinguishable from 'his men'... Once there were rifle shots far away on the left and the commandant leapt up and bellowed something; then shrugged his shoulders and grinned. 'Tire lapins!' he explained. [Note: Within a month a well-prepared enemy attack took this sector completely by surprise and advanced several miles towards Madrid. P.T.]

Back at the Frente it was cold as usual and I suddenly felt utterly tired and bored; I wished I was back in the luxury of Ganthorpe. [Note: My parents' house in Yorkshire. P.T.]

December 27th. We went to the Casa de Campo and up to the second line. There was a young German colonel with a very pretty Spanish wife. She held classes for the illiterate members of the regiment – the great majority – and these were regularly though voluntarily attended whenever the men came back from action. On into the front line trenches were mortar-bombs falling behind and in front of us, and I took one shot, through sandbags, at the flitting figure of a Moor between the ruins. Felt mildly afraid, but also exhilarated...

...[In the University City] there was a dog in the trench whom they'd nicknamed 'Franco' because he regularly dined with us but ran across to have lunch with the fascists. One day he'd returned from the enemy lines with a bit of cardboard attached to his neck, on which was written: 'I am a red soldier who will pass over to your lines as soon as he can. Salud, Camerad!' [Note: I kept this treasured document for thirty years afterwards, but it seems to have disappeared at last. P.T.]

A wounded man was carried in and I went and stood behind a wall, watching soldiers running doubled-up across a dangerous gap... two boys of about sixteen hitching bandoliers over their shoulders and walking resolutely down to the barricades. And what a shit I felt, leaning elegantly against the wall with a glass of wine in my hand and watching these others do the fighting... We were shown a smiling young Moor who had deserted and a bearded French machine-gunner who had refused promotion three times...

...spoke on the wireless and was told that my voice was like a mixture of Edward VIII and Baldwin!

A reception given by the adjutant of the 5th regiment; a very impressive Alsatian. How I *like* that aquiline Party face which one meets in every country, the hard lines and the amazingly clear eyes. I can tell, now, whether a person is in the Party or not, at least after talking to him or her for a few minutes . . .

December 28th. . . . all piled into another bus and left Madrid behind us. Shall I come back? Most unlikely, alas!

Sukup, the tall Czech was getting grumpier and grumpier all night long, and finally I treated him with harsh mockery. I felt a bit ashamed of myself about this; which is odd, as I surely knew that I was right. Or did I? I *do* know that the anti-social must be made social, and that with some people mockery is the best means. But as for my own motives . . .

December 29th. Held a delegation meeting (in Valencia), allotting special subjects to be studied by each member. I was suddenly doubled up with an agonizing stomach cramp, and between two spasms I was rude to G——. A pity, for Liberals ought to be treated with the utmost delicacy . . .

The Party, Perez says, is fighting for religious toleration; but it is unfortunately true that all the churches here have been gutted; and such lovely churches too! Really the Party is having to fight on two fronts at once, against the fascists and against the anarchists; at the same time we get all the blame for anarchist excesses . . . Another striking thing is the Party posters all over the place demanding the safeguarding of peasant proprietors and small shopkeepers. *What* a good party it is!

. . . Frank Pitcairn [Note: pen-name adopted by Claud Cockburn when writing for the *Daily Worker*. P.T.] told us that the Party is trying hard to preserve the existing organizations, even when they're run by kulaks. This is a necessity because the present cooperation of the peasants is absolutely essential. In some places, notably Catalonia, the poorer peasants have expropriated the richer ones, with consequent hostility to the Republican cause . . .

Pitcairn said the present stage was something like N.E.P. [Note: The New Economic Policy, Lenin's tactical retreat in the early twenties, calculated to placate the recalcitrant peasants and lower middle classes. P.T.] The militia is being dissolved and formed into a regular people's army. In fact everything is quieting down a lot now, thanks to Party discipline. Passes are examined on the road by regular police.

Madrid and Valencia, which were loud with shooting every night only a month ago, are quiet now.

And the Party is at last openly turning on the wilder anarchist elements. A few days ago Yague, a Communist youth leader in the Madrid Junta, was murdered in the night. For the first time the Party didn't pretend, for the sake of unity, that this was a fascist shot. They now dare to attack the anarchists openly because the Party is getting stronger and stronger and even has the more sober anarchist elements behind it . . .

Though Pasionaria didn't speak to us except to say 'Salud!' when we first came into the room I found her immensely impressive. And Diaz, the Party's General Secretary, was utterly typical; sunken, thoughtful eyes and a very fine, quiet, modest manner: amazingly young – only 30, Perez told me later . . .

I wasn't quite happy about the Party demand for conscription, and asked whether a conscript army could possibly have the high morale of volunteers. I didn't like having to make this apparent criticism in front of non-p.m.s; especially as the answer wasn't particularly encouraging. I gather conscription is to be adopted out of sheer necessity; with the single consolation that the army will be an admirable field for political education. (65% of the political commissars are Communists!)

After lunch a visit to the Maison de la Culture; a sort of hot-house for intellectuals; rather an irritating place . . .

We visited the Socialists and sat round a regional secretary, firing questions at him. How I wish Chris could have been there [Note: Christopher Mayhew, an anti-communist socialist contemporary at Oxford; later a Labour cabinet minister. P.T.] to hear the disgust they felt for the Second International, and how much they all wanted to join the Third! They quite simply *admitted that they'd been wrong.* (As a matter of fact I suspect that the young man may have been a secret p.m. The only thing which made me doubt this was the directness with which he attacked the Second International.)

December 30th. . . . Gil and I in very high spirits together, screaming with laughter at the absurdity of our whole delegation . . .

New Year's Eve. This day next year what will there be to look back on? I've never before felt so strongly that anything might happen;

that every day brings us visibly nearer to a complete change in our way of life . . .

. . . went to see Del Vayo [Note: Foreign Minister of the Spanish Republic. P.T.] who told us a lot of depressing things about the international situation, but said that the German and Italian military attacks were being held on all fronts. He was absolutely confident of eventual victory and said that Spain was going to emerge as a great nation. (A certain amount of chauvinism here, but on the whole I liked him: a benignity and culture which I found agreeable.)

. . . went to an exhibition of the Duke of Alva's paintings. This was impressive: they'd been saved from Madrid by the 5th Regiment and exhibited all round the cloisters of a monastery. In the middle was a great block of stone, swathed in red-lettered cloth; thanks of the government to the C.P. for their work of preservation . . .

. . . at last got the interview with Caballero [Note: Socialist Prime Minister of the Republic during the early months of the war. P.T.]. A quiet little man, impressive enough but no Spanish Lenin, so I'd guess. He said nothing striking or new but seemed to be capable and reliable. He was a little cynical with us; a little bored by us. I confess I'm surprised that more people aren't!

After that I hurried poor Perez all over the place trying to get permission to visit a prison. This was partly because of M's [Note: my mother's. P.T.] rather gleeful discovery of the M.P.s' statement that they'd been shown only ten prisoners all the time they were in Madrid.* I've asked several people about this, and it seems to be sheer nonsense. It's a definite and established thing that prisoners *are* taken. An Italian airman was brought down the other day and couldn't understand it when he wasn't shot. Most of the Madrid prisoners are moved out of the city at once because of the food shortage. Indeed I'd be *amazed* if prisoners were shot, because this would be directly contrary to government policy in other matters; its refusal, for example, ever to bombard open towns. The side that has the people behind it would naturally have a completely different policy from the side that is attempting to impose the will of a small minority.

Anyway we couldn't get an authorization in the two hours that were left to us in Valencia; which was annoying but hardly surprising.

* A recent delegate of British M.P.s who had visited Republican Spain and produced a hostile report of what they'd seen.

However they were anxious for us to come the next day, and sorry to hear that we wouldn't be here then . . .

A farewell coffee with Perez. What a nice, conscientious, unassuming person he has proved to be: all that a rank-and-file p.m. *should* be. I only wish the millions of people who still think of Communists as bloody ogres could come to Spain and see what they're really like . . .

New Year's Day: 1937. I woke up on the hard seat of the train and found that the dawn had just begun. So I called Gil out to the open part of the carriage and we watched a red ball of sun creep out of the sea for the first day of 1937 . . . There were trenches between the sea and the railway-line, and I must admit I was quite glad to think that they were the last I'd see for some time . . .

Barcelona has the gaiety of a Mediterranean port, but I didn't feel quite as I had when we were here before. The C.N.T. was very much in evidence, and there was an uncomfortable feel of anarchy in the air. Alas, it is really a creed for the *Lumpenproletariat*, and many of the F.A.I. [Note: *Federación Anarquista Ibérica.* P.T.] look lumpen as lumpen could be. Also I now felt intensely irritated by the gutted churches. It's clearly true that the priests used them as arsenals and fortresses; but this is no excuse for a revolutionary party indulging in the wanton destruction of beautiful buildings. And of course to M and Co it is all the work of 'communists'! Bugger the bloody C.N.T. and their *enfantillages*!

I felt as I never felt even in Madrid – that shooting might break out at any minute. And yet I couldn't help liking most of the people in the street . . .

In any case when we went to visit the H.Q. of the Socialist youth movement we heard highly encouraging news about the growth of the U.G.T. at C.N.T. expense. If only we can keep them working with us until Franco is beaten we shall be able to deal with them easily enough after the war is over. I mean through our numerical superiority . . .

January 3rd. I'd bought Gide's *Retour de L'U.R.S.S.* at the Gare St Lazarre, and read it between Paris and Dieppe. A really alarming book, because written by an obviously sympathetic and sensitive person, yet devastating in criticism which rings unquestionably true.

Complacency; complete lack of freedom of thought; the recrudescence of class . . .

I'm afraid I simply *believe* this account, even without reservations. We must, MUST do something about it: protest, first, against the Trotskyist label which is immediately attached to any critic of the Soviet Union; then try to extort a reply from the Soviet Government. (All this, of course, inside the Party.)

* * *

Before letting the commentator loose on this tempting material it might be as well to give his own credentials: where he stands now as he delivers his judgements and retrospective glosses on the text of his predecessors; what, as briefly as possible, he has done and thought, written, felt and believed since he left the communist party in the late summer of 1939.

A brisk survey reveals, alas, a figure who has continued to be almost comically representative, almost grotesquely a figure of his own age, country, class and sub-class. (As a *writer* this may well be a great advantage to him; and indeed he has long been engaged on a book which would have been called *A Hero of Our Time* if the title hadn't already been used by Lermontov. But as a man it is hard not to feel a certain irritation when I realize that I have so faithfully reproduced the successive moods, aversions and inclinations of 'the' left-wing English intellectual, 1939 to 1976.)

A bad war, fought, and was this rather feebly, against the British rather than the German army. Although I had played so little direct part in it I think I felt that *my* war was the one which had been lost at last in the spring of 1939; and lost, what's more, partly because of the actions and inactions of many who were still in the British government. The Labour victory in 1945 stirred up old hopes again, but these were quickly dashed, whether justifiably or not, by the record of the new government in the later forties. From then until 1956 I was less politically inclined than I had ever been, retiring with satisfaction into the raising of a second family and the secret planning of a monstrous book. I never moved to the right, according to familiar expectations; but when I looked at the domestic or the international scene I usually did so with boredom, irritation or revulsion.

It was the Suez outrage of 1956 which brought me suddenly out of this comatose political and social state and back into a public rage again. After that I served my time in C.N.D., but without winning any medals; groaned, but not very loudly, under successive Conservative governments, and welcomed the return of Labour in 1964 with controlled enthusiasm. In the spring of 1957 I had even organized, and occasionally participated in, a banner-bearing pilgrimage from Manchester to Strasbourg which proclaimed the disgust of its two to twenty marchers both at the British bombing of Egypt and at the Russian reoccupation of Hungary.

Meanwhile, and indeed for the whole of my adult life, I had been searching for some kind of religious faith, and had slowly discovered that I was now in a position where, as I wrote in 1966, it would be a little less misleading to say that I believed in God than to say that I did not. Scarcely a Damascus Road conversion, but a cautious advance from a dissatisfied agnosticism to an uncertain and precarious faith.

And then, in the early seventies, the almost inevitable lurch into the cause of conservation and survival; of the small community; the devolution of power . . . A fairly articulate doomsman, I began to question many of my long-held 'progressive' assumptions, moving, so I firmly believe, resolutely to the left of any position I had ever occupied before. Associating more and more with young men and women who had dropped out of contemporary society, I even took a leading part in the foundation of an organic farming community in a house where I had lived with my family for the previous fourteen years. I even wore a promising Tolstoyan beard for a few sagacious months in the summer of 1974.

And now?

Now the commentator would describe himself as a full-blown anarchist, a near-pacifist and an unorthodox Christian. This, approximately, is the position from which he looks back, in 1976, on the communist student of forty years ago. If he lives for many more years it seems unlikely, from his past record, that he will stay in exactly the same spot. But some things at least can be said with total conviction: I shall continue to be a radical egalitarian, as I have been at least since the age of seventeen; I shall continue to believe, as I have increasingly believed since I left the communist party, that a political and social revolution without an accompanying moral, spiritual and psychological revolution will be useless at best, and perhaps a good deal worse than useless.

* * *

Equipped and limited by this biography and these beliefs I shall now begin my commentary on the passages I have quoted from the diary of 1936. (The use of the third person for my earlier self is not meant to imply a radical separation of the two narrators; it is simply a device for reducing confusion of the two periods in the mind of the reader.)

'... *the all-too-rare approbation of my Party*...' But for this revealing phrase, and a hint or two elsewhere, it would be hard for a reader to guess that the student-delegate got into as many scrapes with his bosses and equals in the C.P.G.B. as he had got into at his many schools and as he would soon be getting into in the British army. He was held to be a bourgeois deviationist of almost corkscrew propensities; it was held vigorously against him that he liked to drink too much and to get into bed with as many girls as would allow him to do so. But *fundamentally* it was generally believed that he was sound; he certainly believed this himself, as nearly all the following passages will show.

The manipulations of the party in Paris are taken so much for granted by now – after just over a year's membership – that no comment seems to have been needed.

The Catalan coast. The student delegate's descriptions of scenery are perfunctory in the extreme, and nearly all of them tinged (red) by the pathetic fallacy that '... our people are fighting for our things...' But in fact very few young English communists knew anything at all about Spain. They adored their own pipe-dream of the Soviet Union; they loved to plot in Paris; they sang American Union songs, and they were deeply conscious of German and Italian fascism. But this easy assumption that those who were fighting the Spanish Civil War on the government side were closely akin to communist students at Oxford shows an almost ludicrous ignorance of Spanish history and the Spanish reality of 1936. Yet I find that this illusion, or at least partial illusion, still has power to move me. There is an old, faintly ludicrous but largely admirable tradition of Englishmen attaching themselves to the revolutionary struggles of foreign peoples. Byron is the most famous example; and for all his glaring and self-advertised faults Byron's life and death in Greece have rightly haunted the imagination of Europe ever since.

'*. . . even Trotskyists could be nice in this country.*' This must surely read like a monstrous example of communist naivety; in fact it is an almost heroic act of generosity and intelligence. For what the party had instilled into him, with demoniac zeal (perhaps above every other act of indoctrination), was that Trotsky and his followers were as vile as the fallen angels in hell. The trials had already begun in Russia; Trotsky's machinations had been discovered behind almost every 'conspiracy', and no heresy was more abominable than to show even the faintest tinges of sympathy for anything that this arch-fiend had ever done or said or written.

Huesca! A name which still shines through the subsequent murk for many of us, if only because of John Cornford's moving little poem. (Cornford was an admired Cambridge comrade, who was killed outside Madrid in the middle of the narrator's own brief visit to Spain.)

TO MARGOT HEINEMANN

Heart of the heartless world,
Dear heart, the thought of you
Is the pain at my side,
The shadow that chills my view.

The wind rises in the evening,
Reminds that autumn is near.
I am afraid to lose you,
I am afraid of my fear.

On the last mile to Huesca,
The last fence of our pride,
Think so kindly, dear, that I
Sense you at my side.

And if bad luck should lay my strength
Into the shallow grave,
Remember all the good you can;
Don't forget my love.

'*Copain espagnol*', the first of many French phrases which seem to have no particular French point. I think the explanation must be that he had spent many exciting 'revolutionary' days in Paris that summer, during the honeymoon of the newly elected Popular Front government of Léon Blum. (Later Blum was loathed by most of the international left wing for his leading part in the hypocritical Anglo-French 'non-intervention' policy.)

'*. . . not much of an ammunition shortage!*' Sancta Simplicitas! I would now ascribe these gestures to the natural ebullience and open-handedness of the anarchist mentality: for better or for worse they are not the kind of people who count the cost or look before they leap.

'*This is a workers' city at war . . .*' Yes, it is perfectly true that the anarchist workers really had taken over this large Mediterranean port; and nearly everybody who visited Barcelona in those early months of the Civil War came away with the same almost ecstatic sense of old and bad things put away, new and splendid things begun. Here is Franz Borkenau, a case-hardened, ex-communist journalist from Central Europe: 'Few people in the Casa de Colon. And then as we turned round the corner of the Ramblas came a tremendous surprise: before our eyes in a flash, unfolded itself the revolution. It was overwhelming. It was as if we had been landed on a continent different from anything I had seen before . . .'

This is the scene that has stayed forever in my mind, almost as clearly as when I first saw it. 'Bliss was it in that dawn to be alive, But to be young was very heaven.' Whenever I have been tempted to fall into political cynicism I remember the joyful militia of Barcelona, many of them still in civilian clothes but with bandoliers slung over their shoulders. I remember all the commandeered private cars, and how you could hail any car, ask for a lift to anywhere in the city and get it with a smile. The whole city has stayed in my mind as one great grin of amazed delight; the delight of liberty, fraternity and equality really in action (and the greatest of these is fraternity).

Of course I know now that this joyful state of affairs has never lasted long. I know the bitter lessons of revolutionary history, and though I am now myself an anarchist I cannot believe that even those great-hearted anarchists of Catalonia could have kept that grin on the face of their city forever and ever. There was a war on their hands, and not even the anarchists doubted that it had to be fought. The communists were already beginning to chivy them into a betrayal of their fundamental principles. Nor was this in itself a wicked or even, by ordinary standards, a misguided policy. Advancing against Franco's machine-guns in cheering waves, without either officers or military organization of any kind, the anarchists had suffered terrible losses and achieved almost nothing. Some of them were already drawing the lesson that they must imitate a communist style of organization; none of them, that I know of, concluded that true anarchy may well be incompatible with fighting any kind of war.

But there, in 1936, on the Ramblas of Barcelona, the Spanish anarchists had their finest hour. Nobody can tell, now, whether they might have achieved a new kind of society if there had been no war and no communists to harry them into order, even to kill them if they refused to be harried. Those who accept the doctrine of original sin will never believe that anarchists have enjoyed some sort of immaculate conception which spares them from that congenital sickness of the will which frustrates the rest of us. My own present belief is that true anarchism corresponds to something quite as deep in human nature as greed, selfishness and aggression. I am no utopian; I see no prospect of any heaven being built on this earth; but the suppression and defeat of the Spanish anarchists now seems to me to be one of the major political tragedies of our time. It is good to know that there are still anarchists in Spain, undefeated, after all, in the sense that they have never been defeated by despair.

'*Very tired and late . . . there was a splendid air of efficiency about this place . . .*' The leader of this student delegation must have been reasonably efficient himself, for not only had he been chosen for this job by his party, but he was also, by now, the chairman of the Organising Committee (Org. Com.) of the Oxford University branch of the C.P. But was it *natural* in him to esteem this quality so highly, or was this, too, a result of fourteen months' indoctrination?

I think it was natural to him. Certainly I have seldom, in later life, surrendered to the dubious charms of inefficiency. When I have witnessed it at its most acute – in the Arab countries of the Middle East – I have always been struck by the burdens and discomforts of living in a society which is both corrupt and incompetent. When I stayed for a few days on board a British destroyer in the Mediterranean I was deeply impressed by the leisure and good living provided by a service which was a great deal more efficient than anything I had ever come across in my chequered army career. Nor do I see any reason why an anarchist ought to prefer that his small community should run itself badly. What pleasure or honour is there, for example, in being a lazy and incompetent farmer?

'*... and soon we were in the middle of a delightful party...*' This is one of the fairly few occasions in a remarkably priggish text when P.T.'s Old Adam takes a quick look through his raised vizor. Not many communists were puritans in the strict sense of the word; indeed great attention was paid to love affairs and strong views were expressed about the 'correctness' of partaking in them, even of enjoying them. But the girls were supposed to be party members too; an affair that the diarist briefly and headily conducted with a 'bourgeois' girl was viewed with great suspicion by his comrades. And rightly too, for he sometimes entertained his girlfriend with hilarious accounts of the more preposterous aspects of party life.

'... not, *we were assured, molested...*' The raping of nuns was a favourite theme of pro-Franco propaganda all over the world. To this day I haven't the slightest idea how widespread this odd practice was among Spanish revolutionaries; but my avatar's blind acceptance of such a bland assurance is all too reminiscent of those constant visitors to Soviet Russia during the worst of the Terror who came back with rosy reports of heroic justice done to black-hearted traitors; a new and glorious society being built; Stalin the Father of his People... A nauseating record of wilful credulity, to which I here contribute my own little morsel of dung.

'*The militiamen were so universally nice...*' An adjective more suited to Oxford tea parties, perhaps, than to the rough realities of a civil war. But the sense of fellowship was genuine enough, however superficial. In spite of many early defeats there was still unbounded confidence on the Republican side that the war would be won before long, if only by the will and joy of the people. Although the Spaniards knew almost nothing about these students and their exotic backgrounds, and the students knew no more about the Spaniards, yet there *was*, at the very least, a common happiness and a common hope. For although this was technically a defensive war, and would prove to be a dismal and almost unrelieved sequence of Republican defeats, it was also felt by anarchists, socialists and communists alike to be the effective beginning of a gallant revolution.

It is a foolish cynicism to believe that because a human emotion is impermanent it is therefore derisory. Few people can stay for long at the most ecstatic pitch of being in love, yet it is generally agreed that this brief and doomed emotion is a major human experience, and among the most enlightening of them all. Certainly I regret nothing of the affection and admiration I felt for those Spanish soldiers.

'*... murder of party leaders by anarchists ...*' This may have happened, but the verdict of history is surely that it was the Communist Party which took the initiative in the internecine butcheries of Civil War years. There was a very particular loathing, among many communists, for anybody who could make a reasonable claim to be standing to the left of their own party. By definition the Communist Party was the only legitimate far Left; by definition it was the ultimate band in the spectrum. Therefore anyone who claimed that he rejected the party from the left of it was clearly a liar and a mountebank; probably a disguised fascist. Anarchists were never so deep in the party demonology as Trotskyists, but they were a perpetual affront – and, in the end, an affront which could no longer be tolerated.

'*... and then presumably leave the peasants as uneducated as they are today.*' Mixed feelings about this. I still believe that there is no present way in which underdogs can escape from their servitude except by the dubious path of conventional education, yet I also feel deeply suspicious of the condescending attitude which this sentence suggests. I don't know whether there can be such a thing as 'pure' education, education which has no other motive or function except to free and encourage the fullest potential of the human spirit. I don't know whether Ivan Illich's hopes of de-schooling society make any real sense or not. But I strongly suspect that what I meant by 'education' during my communist years was something which I would now call indoctrination.

'*Quite suddenly we could see the whole of Madrid lying in front of us ...*' Here and in many other passages there is a strong whiff of the student delegate's excitable and romantic attitude to war. Born in 1916, his whole childhood had been luridly coloured by stories of the First World War; and in adolescence he had read, with equivocal passion, the new anti-war memoirs of Graves, Sassoon and others. As a communist he had already helped to organize many an 'anti-war' campaign, constantly insisting on the peaceful nature and intentions of Soviet Russia, the inevitable bellicosity of capitalism. 'War is hell' was a slogan which he and his comrades had been taught to parrot.

But I think most of them had remained emotionally unconvinced. The Somme, Passchendaele, Verdun . . . they knew perfectly well, of course, that these were terrible names and that unspeakably terrible things had been happening at those places during their infancy. Yet how they wished that they themselves had witnessed and survived those horrors! 'War is hell' induced a romantic frisson all its own, and every bit as violent as 'War is glory'. For who can honestly say that he finds heaven more interesting than hell, eternal bliss of better value than everlasting torment?

I believe that half the excitement the narrator felt on his brief journey through Spain was the excitement of attending a war. The fact that it was a revolutionary war made it that much more thrilling, of course, but I suspect that any war would have been better than none.

'*Splendid people . . . Josefina Lopez.*' A heady atmosphere indeed: the besieged city which had become a universal symbol of the people at bay; these hardened communists nomads of Europe, truly splendid in their courage, in their humour, in their undefeated hopes for a better world; and a pretty girl on top of the cake! What more could a romantic young man have asked?

What more would I ask today?

Well, I would ask for some appreciation that a besieged city is also a bitterly suffering city. I would ask that these admirable communists should have had deeper suspicions than any they had yet shown that their God had already failed and that their revolution had been betrayed from the very top. As for Josefina, I still applaud the emotions I felt then and the amorous plans which must have been seething in my head.

'*Until now I had never really* felt *about the bombing and shelling of an open city . . .*' About time too! But the end of the paragraph is surely another example of pitiful simplicity. People who have been 'shelled to pieces' have usually proved remarkably easy to govern.

'*I suppose there's nowhere in the world a more admirable group of men than these gallant 15,000 . . .'* A wild overestimation of the size of the International Brigade in those early months, but I see no reason at all to retract my admiration. True that few young and idealist volunteers in any war have fully understood the horrors, miseries and boredoms that await them. But at least the great majority of these young, and older, men were aware that to fight meant risking their lives and their limbs. And nearly all of them certainly believed that they were fighting for a great and good cause against a cruel and brutish one. (At least the second of these beliefs has survived the ironies of history.)

'I felt absurdly miserable and moved . . .' But today I am a little suspicious of these constant claims that his was the harder part, and that he would have stayed to fight if the party had only allowed him to do so. His later life, and particularly in wartime, suggests that he was more of a Sancho Panza than a Don Quixote, a natural survivor rather than the kind of young man whose name looks appropriate on a war memorial.

General Kléber. I have heard nothing since then which suggests that this admiration was misplaced. Those who have read such horrific accounts of Stalinist Russia as Nadezhda Mandelstam's *Hope against Hope* may find it hard to believe that any Soviet official at that time could still have had any faith left in the virtue of his party and his government. But there were many who hoped against hope in a different sense from Mrs Mandelstam's. So much faith and work and courage had been sunk in that cause by good and honourable men; is it any great wonder that very few of them were able to face the monstrous fact of betrayal until they themselves had had their noses pushed into the filth of the Terror! Some of them even survived a full personal experience of the Camps and continued to serve the cause which had tortured them and killed their friends.

There is a type of self-righteous Westerner who revels in condemning the 'cowardice' or worse of men like Kléber; but the only reason why most of those facile despisers would never have acted as he did is that they would never have been capable of his faith and generosity. By Christmas 1936 the communist cause was a bad cause; it was still served by many good men.

' "*Tire lapins!*" ' Whatever the cause I still prefer bad soldiers to good ones, just as, whatever the cause, I still prefer those who support it with a certain irony, even clownishness, to those who are sternly and humourlessly dedicated to its unremitting service. Yes, these French volunteers lost valuable ground because they preferred shooting rabbits to shooting (inedible) fascists. But that admirable preference remains a fine thing in itself, quite unaffected, to my present way of thinking, by the results to which it led.

In Malraux's *Days of Hope*, one of the better of a bad lot of Spanish war novels, the anarchist is defined as a man who wants to *be* something, the communist as a man who wants to *do* something. At that time Malraux preferred the doer, and so did I. Today I doubt whether it's any use trying to do anything on a large scale until one has first taken the trouble – a long and painful trouble for most of us – to become the sort of man who is capable of wise and fruitful action. The rabbit shooters were undoubtedly communists, not anarchists, but in this piece of noble frivolity they showed themselves to be anarchists at heart.

'*... wished I was back in the luxury of Ganthorpe.*' An honest *cri de coeur*, for this young member of the English upper middle classes had lived a very pampered life by the standards of the wider world. Nor had he, in any significant sense, abandoned his own class when he joined the communist party. True, he spent some of his vacation from Oxford either selling the *Daily Worker* on the streets of that city, or living and working (politically) with unemployed miners in South Wales, or attending international conferences of 'Anti-fascist Youth'. But he was still firmly based on his old Yorkshire home, constantly visiting Castle Howard, a mile away, where his uncle presided benignly over large house parties of his cousins and their friends.

But even if this young man was indeed having the best of both worlds I still think he did better than most of his school and college associates, who had the best of only one.

'*... I took one shot, through sandbags, at the flitting figure of a Moor between the ruins.*' But this is a different kind of frivolity from that of the *tireurs de lapins*, and not a kind which I admire. For what, after all, was the motive of this visitor to a war in taking a pot shot at a 'Moor'? (This derogatory word was much used in our propaganda, and we constantly protested, in shocked and indignant tones, that Franco had introduced African barbarians into a European war. Curious, now, to think how little part the realities of imperialism and colonial oppression played in the left-wing imagination of the thirties.)

Certainly he didn't borrow this rifle and fire this shot through the trees because he believed that by doing so he was serving the cause of the Spanish Republic; even the raw militiaman whose rifle he had taken would surely have had a better chance of hitting the target than a young man who had been the prime buffoon of his Officers' Training Corps at school.

No, what he wanted was to be able to say, when he got home, that he had shot off at least one bullet in battle: better still that he had killed at least one enemy soldier. He would have done better, I now think, to have joined the rabbit hunt than to have played at war like a little boy trying to knock down lead soldiers.

'*How I like that aquiline Party face . . .*' It is often said, by those who have thought little or badly about the whole topic, that there is not much to distinguish communists from fascists. For these observers the Spanish Civil War can be dismissed as a struggle between two equally plaguey houses; whoever the victors had been, the victims would certainly have been the Spanish people. The second of these propositions may well be true, for it is as sure as any historical might-have-been can be that if the Republican alliance had won the war the communist party would soon have been in total control of the country, whatever fig-leaf they had plastered across their private intentions. And we know the lot of 'the people' in postwar 'people's democracies'.

But the student delegate's piece of naive, and indeed fascist-sounding, hero worship at this point in his narrative is an exception which proves a stranger rule. The fact is that few if any of my working class communist friends had 'that aquiline Party face', and most of them would have made derisive fun of me if they had come across this passage in my journal. Harry Pollitt, the General Secretary of the Communist Party of Great Britain during my whole period as a member, had the rough-and-ready face of an English boilermaker, which is what he was, and bore no resemblance whatever to an eagle-like 'leader of men'. Whatever his faults – and he certainly had the usual human quota – he never decked himself out as any sort of mystical Fuehrer figure; if only because he never lost his sense of humour.

Since the Spanish war *can*, in the light of later history, be roughly simplified into a war between communists and fascists, this is a point which needs to be pursued a little further. Certainly there was something in common between the reality of Stalin's Russia and the reality of Hitler's Germany. I think first, and perhaps rather trivially, of the Soviet pavilion in the Paris International Exhibition of 1936, and of the two gigantic and heroic figures, male and female, who bore their banners on its prow. We all know about the common barbarities of the two countries, the common worship of a leader. But even here there are distinctions to be made, not necessarily in favour of Soviet Russia but in favour of historical and analytical accuracy. Those who experienced both the Russian and the German Terrors have commented that whereas the Germans often killed and tortured with a kind of sacred joy the Russians usually did so with a dull and brutish indifference. And as for the cult of the Leader, it is certain that Hitler worshipped himself with every bit as much ardour as he was worshipped by the great majority of Germans. Stalin, on the other hand, was partly a cynical manipulator who deliberately exploited his own cult, and partly a paranoiac who genuinely believed that he was surrounded by potential assassins.

And even if there were superficial resemblances in the thirties between Russia and Germany there were few if any between the general atmosphere of communism outside Russia and fascism outside Germany. Search the whole of England and it would have been hard to find two more dissimilar men than Harry Pollitt and Sir Oswald Mosley. And anyone who had taken part in London street fights between Blackshirts and communist workers – the student delegate had done so on many occasions – would have known that the combatants were as different from each other as a cloth cap is different from a four-inch wide leather belt with a brass buckle.

It is true, of course, that some fascists became communists and some communists became fascists, but these defectors were either cynics joining the more powerful group, or a small minority of sad drifters searching in vain for a home.

The real difference between the two forces – the ultimate though almost unrecognized rationale at least of the strong international element in the Spanish Civil War – was the ancient spiritual and intellectual conflict between Classicism and Romanticism. However much the student delegate was himself impelled by romantic emotions the movement which he served had descended, via Karl Marx, from the Enlightenment of the eighteenth century. Stalinist Russia represented a gross perversion of the belief that everything can be ordered by reason;

that if 'superstition' is stamped out and if men are shown where their true interests lie, then a rational and humanly satisfying order will quickly be created. Fascism, on the other hand, was a direct and often conscious descent from the Romantic movement, via, among many others, Nietzsche and Wagner. Romanticism gone bad becomes worship of darkness, death and suffering; contempt for common sense; the irrational urges of 'the blood' and 'the soil' elevated to first principles of action. Classicism gone bad becomes the equation of reason with the ruthless elimination of all 'unreasonable' elements.
and didn't care whether they killed or not. Only a very few of the

Decent communists killed because they believed that killing was a horrible necessity; vile communists killed because they were told to Russian killers seem to have done so with rapture.

As for the German camps, there were of course many 'conventional' bureaucrats who supervised the killing in much the same spirit as they would have supervised the running of a gigantic baby creche. But the very title of the extermination policy – *Nacht und Nebel*, 'Night and Mist' – shows with the utmost clarity what *Walpurgisnacht* lay deepest in its origins. Nor is it possible to imagine that if the Germans had surrounded Moscow, Stalin, Molotov and Voroshilov would have immolated themselves on a Wagnerian pyre.

Reason carried to madness had shown its horrors long before, during the last months of Robespierre's Terror. Romanticism pressed downwards into nihilism had glittered in the appalling figure of Nechaev, and in the creatures partly based on him, who loom through the pages Romantic vision would be a world grossly deprived, so a world of *The Possessed*. Just as a world which lacked the Classical or dominated by either spirit in full corruption is bound to be a hell on earth. But no good is served by confusing corrupted reason with corrupted imagination.

'*. . . the anti-social must be made social . . .*' This has a very ugly ring in the light of what we know now, and should have known then, about the fanaticism of all utopians. But I am quite sure that the student delegate was not thinking of the Gulag Archipelago as a suitable treatment for anti-social forces. Indeed, to do him justice, he had already begun to ask awkward questions about the Moscow trials – always, of course, within the bosom of the party – and had been rapped over the knuckles for his scruples.

But there is a very unpleasant priggishness about this passage, which is only slightly relieved by the expressed suspicion that all may not be well with the motives behind it. It is impossible to be doctrinaire without being a prig, and I have found this to be as true of Freudians as it is of dogmatic Christians, as true of logical positivists and linguistic analysts as it is of Marxists. Once a mind has closed, every thought which conflicts with it must be either wicked or contemptible.

'*... Liberals ought to be treated with the utmost delicacy...*' He was quite capable of simple Machiavellian calculations; in fact he and his comrades took a good deal of pleasure from their more or less successful manipulation of potential allies. In the Oxford politics of the Labour Club, the League of Nations Union and the Student Christian Movement this seems little worse than ludicrous. It was much worse than ludicrous for the allies of the East European communist party who were gulped down or slowly devoured during the later 1940s.

'*Kulaks*': how strange it sounds in later ears, the jargon of the day before yesterday! I note that my friend Claud Cockburn, more than ten years older than me and much wiser in the ways of the party, made no attempt to hide the difference between communist tactics and communist aims. *Il fallait reculer pour mieux sauter*: and whose throat would the wolf have jumped at if he'd had the chance? Well, certainly at the throat of the unfortunate 'kulak', if only for a start.

Pasionaria and Diaz: Dolores Ibarruri, known everywhere as La Pasionaria (the Passion Flower), first uttered the famous (but as it transpired false) phrase – *No Pasarán!*, 'They shall not pass'. She was far and away the most colourful communist in Spain, and the best orator. Her later, strictly conformist career suggests that in power she might well have become just such another gorgon as the Rumanian Anna Pauker. José Díaz, on the other hand, was a quiet and self-effacing man, but one with a will and conscience of his own. Like so many communists of that type and style he was later to disappear in Russia, and 'in mysterious circumstances'.

'*I wasn't quite happy about the Party demand for conscription...*' Good! But the worry comes oddly, all the same, from one who accepted so much in the way of direction, discipline and worse. Did he still believe, even then, that official communism was a kind of libertarianism; that the state was due to wither away as soon as Stalin could get round to blighting it?

'*. . . Gil and I in very high spirits . . .*' Another welcome moment of relief from the general earnestness, reinforced a few paragraphs later by his ready acceptance of the Spanish Prime Minister's impatience with him and his companions. In fact a good many young communists of the thirties were capable of much more self-mockery than history has given them credit for. Here, for what the recherché information is worth, there was a most conspicuous difference between Oxford and Cambridge communists. At Oxford we delighted in such blasphemous songs as 'Stalin is my darlin'' or 'I'm the Man who Blows up Railway Trains for Hitler' (based on 'The Man who Broke the Bank at Monte Carlo', and a scorchingly incredulous comment on the 'confessions' delivered by the old Bolsheviks at their state trials in Moscow). Our Cambridge comrades were outraged by such frivolities, but we remained more or less unrepentant, at least so long as my earlier self had any influence on the tone of the Oxford University Communist Party. Disgusted by the absurdity of certain slogans which he had been encouraged to shout while marching on demonstrations ('playing fields; not Battle fields!' 'Footballs; not cannon Balls!'), he had substituted his own derisive versions ('Legal Abortions; not Air-raid precautions!' 'Masturbation; not Mass Starvation!').

But this is to wander a long way from Spain on New Year's Eve. Here again I am moved to a certain respect for my avatar. Hope is a Christian virtue, though it never seems to rank so high as its two more famous associates, and this was one quality with which we were well supplied indeed. Even though our specific hopes were nearly all disappointed, even derided, I am still glad that I once experienced that heady emotion in such a rich profusion. I am glad of this not because I now have no hopes left but because I learned the habit of hoping when I was young and have never altogether abandoned it.

'*This day next year what will there be to look back on?*' Well, there would be almost continuous defeats in Spain; Mussolini's total suppression of Abyssinia; the formation of the Rome-Berlin Axis; the final preparations for Hitler's occupation of Austria . . . These were not years in which it was *shrewd* to be politically hopeful.

'*. . . trying to get permission to visit a prison . . .*' The following passage is perhaps the most distressingly remarkable in the whole of his Spanish diary. What further comment does it need – except the rather wan reminder that there are still preposterous self-deceivers among the politically naive and immature; and particularly among those obstinately repetitious and raucous young left-wingers who persist in believing that *their* bloody revolution will be different and better than any that ever happened before it.

The student delegate wanted so much to believe that those who fought for the Spanish Republic were all good and noble men, though none so good, noble and practical as the communists. It seems that when he was in this state anybody could have fobbed him off with anything. A nun being raped in the open street? Oh, part of a carnival! A scene from an open-air 'People's Theatre'! Or else the lady suffered, poor dear, from a strange perversity; and who but a kindly communist militiaman would have had the courtesy to satisfy it at such a risk to his own reputation? 'Indeed I'd be *amazed* if nuns were raped unless they wanted to be, because this would be directly contrary to the Government's policy in other matters.'

'*Barcelona has the gaiety of a Mediterranean port, but . . .*' Only ten days have passed since the revolutionary ecstasy he felt and expressed when he was last in this city. Constant association with communists, abetted by his own peculiar conscience, had now persuaded him to resist the heady attractions of an anarchist city. I find both the anger and the superiority which he exhibits in this passage intensely disagreeable. Even John Cornford, dead just five days on the morning of the student delegate's return to Barcelona, had embraced the anarchists in his general love of the revolutionary cause; and up to his death there was no more fanatical party member than he.

There is a meanness of disposition about this rejection which was not, I think, natural to the writer and may fairly be ascribed to the narrow jealousies and the intransigent quest for total power which were among the nastiest faults of the communist party.

'*And yet I couldn't help liking most of the people in the street . . .*' 'Lumpen as lumpen' though they were! But still, a wistful sign of grace. Just as a final one is provided by the last entry of all.

'*Gide's Retour de l'U.R.S.S.*' At this time André Gide was the most influential writer in France. After many intellectual and spiritual gyrations he had plumped for communism a few years earlier, though never for membership of the communist party. But unlike so many fellow-travellers of those years he had kept his wits about him on the obligatory visit to Russia and had looked at more than he was shown. His little report was written more in sorrow than in anger, which made it an all the more devastating indictment.

One of the immediate results of this publication was that Gide was instantly elevated to a prominent place in the communist demonology. And when this particular reader, still saddened and worried by what he had read, *did* indeed raise the question of Gide's report 'inside the Party', his superiors treated him with the usual exasperated contempt: 'Are we going to indulge ourselves in bourgeois intellectual doubts, comrade, or are we going to get on with the job?'

He got on with the job, which now largely consisted, as I have already written, of working for the Spanish Republic in England. It was a decent enough activity, I suppose; collecting dried milk for Spanish children; helping to organize camps for refugee children from the Basque country; trying, by the noisiest possible propaganda, to show that the policy of the Chamberlain government was as mean, cowardly and deceitful towards Spain as it was towards everything else that was happening in Europe . . .

Yet I look back on that long campaign without much enthusiasm; certainly with no social or political nostalgia. An infinite number of committees lasting for an infinite number of hours and achieving infinitely little; the same ranting speeches from platforms all over the country; cunningly devised pamphlets which always told so much less even than the truth we already knew . . . And certain appalling ladies who recruited young men to fight in Spain with as much zest as those martial ladies on the plinths of Trafalgar Square had shown during the First World War. And the Left Book Club books pouring from Mr Gollancz's presses at the rate of at least one a month, most of them worthless, many of them dishonest. Flag-wagging is an unpleasant activity whatever colour the flags may be; and it is no surprise to me now to read in my diary that when my friend Esmond came back on leave to England he was outspokenly disgusted by the atmosphere he found here.

* * *

A highly personal and blinkered account of a very brief visit to the Spanish Civil War, followed by an equally personal commentary from the vantage, or disadvantage, point, of forty years on. It is inevitable that the conclusion which follows will be as personal as all the rest.

Historians will presumably argue indefinitely about that war, and about the 'real' issues that were being fought for. When I consciously simplified the issue into a struggle between fascism and communism I may have concealed as much as I revealed. For just as there were heterogeneous forces fighting together in defence of the Republic so the forces which temporarily united under Franco were to prove almost equally disparate. It is true that during the war itself the Falange (Spanish fascist movement) was the dominant power; but there were also orthodox and traditional monarchists; devout Catholics; generals who cared more for the army than for anything else; and romantic Carlists who longed for a return to an even more impossible past than any of the other Spanish reactionaries.

At the time they all seemed brutes to me, and I never took much interest in making distinctions between them. At least we now know who came out on top after the common victory had been achieved – and it certainly wasn't the Carlists. But though I dislike fascism and military rule as much as I ever did, and though I now dislike corrupt and selfish ecclesiastical hierarchies with even greater intensity than before, yet I can no longer see the Civil War as a simple battle between good and evil.

Whatever was 'really' being fought for I think I know what most of the ordinary soldiers on both sides believed they were fighting for. And many thoughtful historians have recently been converted to the view that what people believed they were doing is at least a very large part of what they *were* doing.

Whether they were communists or Trotskyists, anarchists, socialists or liberals, most of the rank and file on the Republican side certainly believed that they were fighting for the old and irrepressible trinity, liberty, equality and fraternity. Many political analysts and philosophers are convinced that you can have either liberty or equality but never both at the same time. If I believed this myself I would not call myself an anarchist, since anarchism certainly demands both liberty and equality in equal and abundant measure. If I believed that these two were eternally incompatible I suppose I would abandon all social and political attitudes, cultivate my garden with even more ferocity than I do already and firmly refuse to look beyond immediate pleasures and pains, personal love and a private faith. I do not believe that life would be meaningless without any social and political beliefs, but it would surely be greatly reduced in hope and scope.

On the other side I take it that the amalgam of fascists, monarchists and Catholics were united in believing that they were fighting for at least a minimal common programme of social virtues – say order, discipline, natural hierarchy, religion and the deepest Spanish traditions. This is not my favourite constellation of virtues, but I can now (just) recognize that all except one of these *is* a virtue if rightly understood and rightly applied. The notion of 'natural hierarchy' seems to me a barbarous moral vulgarity, perpetuated for thousands of years to preserve illegitimate power and privilege, maintained by a cruel mixture of deception and brute force. But order? Anyone who has witnessed a society in a state of collapse will know that almost any social order is better than the horrors and barbarities of social chaos. Discipline? Whatever the most progressive psychiatrists may say I cannot conceive of a good life which isn't, in some sense, a self-disciplined life. Religion? I am now inclined to believe that without it the human spirit will simply dry up, wither and die. Tradition? Every society has its own good, rich and fruitful traditions, and no society can survive which turns its back on its own history.

Seen in this light the Spanish Civil War does not deserve the mythologizing which immediately followed its conclusion and which is unlikely to be dismantled by any number of new and carefully factual histories. The war was not fought between good men and evil men; it was certainly not fought between kind men and cruel men. It was fought by those who had two vague but distinct visions of man. One vision, true to the general optimism of Rousseau and the Enlightenment, was of men as essentially and innately good, artificially restrained from showing their natural love for each other only by the accidents of an ill-spent history. Even communists, for all the ferocities of their own discipline, were committed to the belief that after a certain period of their own benevolent dictatorship there would be no need for it any longer. In the end they would liberate man from the errors imposed on him by a long history of exploitation; and he would then be fit to manage his own affairs.

Those, on the other hand, who insist on order and discipline as the primary and perennial requirements of a healthy social organization are persuaded, whether altogether consciously or not, that man is indeed a fallen creature, who can be saved from his natural vileness and infamy only by the heavy hand of a wise church and/or a harsh but pure state. As for inequalities of wealth and circumstance, they are as natural as the undeniable and congenital inequalities of virtue and ability.

After more than forty years of adult, though usually desultory, cogitation on these rival and traditional attitudes to human nature I find that I still favour a drastically amended version of the first. Certainly I have always believed that the doctrine of the fall of man is one of the most grotesque and obnoxious ever devised by the perversities of the human imagination.

It is absurd, of course, to announce that 'Man is born good'. Or 'free'. Some babies are born idiots; all are born with horrible tempers and without the least motion of self-control; the primary object of babies and small children is not to give but to get . . . But these obvious biological facts are as far from the absurd notion of original sin – why is it so much harder to accept that we are primitive than to pretend that we are fallen from high estate? – as they are from the egregious Freudian notion that babies are born with ravening and indiscriminate sexual appetites. Babies scream for their food because if they didn't do so they would be in grave danger of not getting it, or at least of not getting it often enough.

Men are not born 'good' or 'bad'; they are born with certain inherited possibilities which may or may not be well and richly developed by their parents, their teachers and themselves. The ancient argument about free will and determinism still continues, but nearly all human beings act on the assumption that they have a certain control over their own destinies, that there are occasions when they deserve to be blamed and others when they deserve to be praised.

And if all this seems a long way from the Spanish Civil War of forty years ago I would answer that every ideological war is ultimately concerned with the ancient issues of ethics, religion and philosophy. Those anarchists of Barcelona, who impressed me so deeply on my first visit to the city, whom I tried but failed to despise on my second visit, were not consciously concerned with free will and determinism, or with original sin and natural virtue. But they not only hoped for the brotherhood of man: but they believed that they themselves were putting this glorious hope into immediate practice. It can hardly be said that they were right about this, for you cannot combine brotherhood with murder – and who can doubt that priests and fascists were being murdered daily and nightly during the fiesta period of Barcelona anarchism.

Still, they had at least achieved a true brotherhood of the poor and afflicted. Ruthless against those whom they rightly regarded as the bitter enemies of such a brotherhood, there was little that they wouldn't do to help one another. Nor should this limited achievement be sneered at as a mere sodality of murderers. It is only by the very highest standards that the anarchists of Catalonia can be condemned for shooting those who had oppressed and exploited them for so long. By any lesser standards what they achieved was truly remarkable; a spontaneous and vital comradeship, an active love of man for man, which survived as long as their communist and fascist enemies permitted it.

I have already suggested that nobody can tell whether this honeymoon would have lasted if nobody had intervened to end it. Probably factions would have grown up among the anarchists of Spain; indeed this actually happened in the course of the war. But for more than a year Barcelona *was*, to a very notable and inspiring extent, a city of comrades; and much of Catalonia witnessed a government of the people, by the people and for the people, such as no capitalist government ever has provided or ever could provide. Although the Spanish anarchists were hopelessly defeated, both by their proclaimed allies and by their open and implacable enemies, they have left behind them a message of limited hope.

It would be absurd not to add that the lesson which many rational and humane people have drawn from the Spanish Civil War is one of almost unlimited despair.

A few years ago I was driving back across Spain from a holiday in Portugal. We skirted the western and northern outskirts of Madrid – my first approach to the city since 1936 – and I was startled by the great high-rise flats which towered above the rubble of the former suburbs, startled still more by suddenly seeing the old haunting names on brash new signposts constructed in the super-modern idiom: Pozuelo; Boadilla; Brunete; Tetua. . . .

I have visited none of the modern holiday resorts in Spain, but my stay in the Algarve was enough to give me an elementary idea of what has happened to the Costa Brava, the Costa del Sol *et al.*

Much has been written both for and against the postwar 'achievements' of the Franco regime, though I confess that I have remained totally unimpressed by even the most cautious and persuasive of the apologists. What cannot be denied is that this regime has utterly and remorselessly betrayed at least one of its deepest original principles. They were fighting, they said, for traditional Spain against the odious foreign materialism of international communism. Whatever we may think of the traditions which were valued most highly by the generals and the bishops, what is now beyond doubt is that traditional Spain, in any meaningful sense of the phrase, has been ruthlessly sacrificed on the twin altars of industrialism and tourism.

Yes, I know all the arguments, and they are powerful ones indeed. If I hate that Spanish tradition which demanded that peasants stay in atrocious poverty while their priests taught them humility and submission, how can I object to innovations which have undoubtedly reduced that poverty, and which even seem to be reducing the dumb acceptance of their lot which defeat in the Civil War had reimposed on the Spanish poor?

The fact is, of course, that in these respects, in his policy of encouraging native industry and developing the tourist trade up to and beyond its maximum capacity, Franco has done belatedly what a communist regime would almost certainly have done a great deal quicker. Only the Carlists and anarchists might have succeeded in keeping Spain out of the modern world, the first by marching rigidly backwards into the nineteenth century, the second by their perception that the modern disease of giantism can be effectively opposed only by maintaining but liberating the small community of the village and the street, the medium-sized community of the region (Catalonia; Andalusia; the Basque country . . .) and the larger, but still natural, confederation of Spain itself.

But even if there was ever a chance that the communists might have defeated the fascists in Spain there was never, at that time, the faintest chance either for the anarchists or for the Carlists. And whichever of the two official sides had won, that side would eventually have set about the task of 'modernizing' Spain in the only way the modern West understands. Whether it had been ruled by Franco or by La Pasionaria, Spain would have joined the twentieth century *on the terms of the twentieth century*. Only the anarchists have been able to keep a paradoxical vision of progress which is also retreat: the perception that there is no reason why a man should starve just because he has kept things human-sized; that a small community, rid of its old oppressors and its new exploiters, can be a much happier place than an industrial suburb or a holiday resort. Only the anarchists really believe that man can rid himself of the cold that comes from rags and hovels without inviting the cold of lost community and lost identity.

L'Espoir was the title of Malraux's Civil War novel, and not even the vulgarities and brutalities of modern Spain can conceal certain elements of present hope. As if by a miracle much of the Spanish Church has become a force for freedom and humanity; students and trade unionists insist on trying to behave like students and trade unionists in countries where they are free to act according to their natures (i.e. both well and badly). Most remarkable of all, there are anarchist communities still perpetuating themselves in modern Spain, managing to put some of their principles into practice even within a state which is still opposed to every one of those principles. Among the many bitter lessons of history one bland old truism still retains its force: while there's life there's hope.

Biographical Notes on Contributors

BASIL COLLIER was working on a book about the Catalan-speaking districts of France during the latter part of the Spanish Civil War. He therefore made several visits to the frontier area and witnessed the bombing of Puigcerdá in 1938. During the Second World War, he served first as an intelligence officer at H.Q., Fighter Command and Supreme H.Q., Allied Expeditionary Forces in Europe, and then as Air Historical Officer, Fighter Command. In 1948 he joined the Cabinet Office as one of the officially appointed military historians of the Second World War. His publications include: *The Defence of the United Kingdom, A Short History of the Second World War* and *Japan at War.*

HUGH THOMAS worked in the Foreign Office from 1954–7 and was Secretary of the U.K. delegation to the U.N. Disarmament sub-committee from 1955–6. He left the Foreign Office in 1957 and became a lecturer at the Royal Military Academy, Sandhurst. From 1960–6 he worked for the U.N. as Director of its Disarmament Campaign. He became Professor of History at Reading University in 1966 and Chairman of the Graduate School of Contemporary European Studies in 1973. His publications include: *The Spanish Civil War, The Selected Writing of José Antonio Primo de Rivera* (editor), *Goya and the Third of May* and *Europe, the Radical Challenge.*

CLAUD COCKBURN became a correspondent of *The Times* in New York and Washington in 1929. Four years later he resigned in order to found his own news-sheet, *The Week.* In 1936 he went to Spain to fight for the Republican cause and to cover the Civil War for the *Daily Worker.* Since 1955, he has written principally for *Punch, New Statesman, Saturday Evening Post* and *Private Eye.* His publications include *Reporter in Spain, Ballantyne's Folly, Bestseller* and *The Devil's Decade.*

BRIAN CROZIER was emotionally but not physically involved in the Spanish Civil War, and joined the Left Book Club in consequence. He began to reassess the outcome of the Civil War in the course of a lengthy reportage on Franco's Spain for the *Economist* in 1955. His biography of Franco, although attacked by the Left, was initially excluded from general distribution in Spain. When a Spanish edition eventually appeared with footnotes critical to the author, it became a best-seller. In 1970 he helped to found the Institute for the Study of Conflict in London. His other publications include biographies of De Gaulle and Chiang-Kai-Shek and *A Theory of Conflict.*

PETER KEMP went to Spain in November 1936 and enlisted with the Carlist Cavalry as a trooper, but was subsequently transferred to the Carlist infantry. He took part in the Jarama battle and also the fighting in the North, in Santander and Asturias. In autumn 1937 he was transferred to the Spanish Foreign Legion, taking part in the battle of Teruel and the Nationalist offensive in March 1938. A serious injury from a mortar bomb put him out of action for the rest of the Civil War. During the Second World War, he fought in the British army in the commandos and the S.O.E. From 1945–6 he worked with the French in Indo-China against the Vietminh communists. He has been a life assurance underwriter since 1951, and covered foreign assignments for various newspapers. His publications include *Mine were of Trouble* (memoirs of the Spanish Civil War), and *Arabian Assignment.*

SHIELA GRANT DUFF was a freelance journalist working in Paris, the Saar and South-Eastern and Central Europe from 1934 to 1939. In 1939 she became Czechoslovak Editor of Foreign Research and Press Section of the Foreign Office, and two years later she was appointed Czechoslovak Editor of the European Service of the B.B.C. Her publications include *Europe and the Czechs* and *A German Protectorate.*

DERRICK FERGUSON went to sea in 1927 as a midshipman, serving in the Atlantic, Mediterranean and South African waters. In 1934 he was appointed Flotilla Signals Officer based on Haifa and the Egyptian ports for the Abyssinian War. At the outbreak of the Spanish Civil War, his flotilla was ordered to protect British interests including merchant shipping, while preserving strict neutrality. During the Second World War he served as a signal officer on a series of ships, and then in the Operations Room of the Admiralty during the invasion of Sicily and Italy by the Allied Forces. After the war he continued his naval career and then served for five years in industry.

ALFRED LENT was editor of one of Berlin's largest newspapers in 1936, when Hitler decreed a compulsory National Service of two years' duration. When the Condor Legion became an open secret, he volunteered for Spain. His subsequent book on his experiences in the Civil War proved a great success when published in 1939. At the outbreak of the Second World War he served on the Eastern front. After the war, he abandoned writing, becoming first a wood carver's apprentice and then a stone mason. In 1952 he emigrated to the U.S.A. working as a commercial artist and industrial scale modelmaker. In 1968 he gave up his full-time occupation at the workbench and is now working as a translator to the British export industry.

KENNETH SINCLAIR-LOUTIT trained as a doctor and in August 1936 went to Spain as Administrator of the field unit sent by the Spanish Medical Aid Committee. In January 1937 this unit was integrated into the 14th International Brigade, seeing action in the Jarama, Las Rosas, and Brunete fronts. During the Second World War he held various posts in medical administration and afterwards became Director of Health and Social Services in the U.N.R.A.A. mission to Yugoslavia. From 1950 to 1961 he worked for W.H.O., first as a medical adviser to UNICEF and then as Chief of Mission in Morocco. He retired in 1973 to live in Rabat where he teaches in the University.

K. P. BOND (see note on pp. 110–111).

J. R. JUMP joined the 15th International Brigade in the autumn of 1937, and saw front-line service with the Britsh Battalion from April to September 1938. During the Ebro offensive he was mentioned in dispatches for bravery. After contracting jaundice he was invalided out of the Spanish army and returned to Britain in December 1938. After serving in the British army during the Second World War, he trained as a teacher and is now Lecturer in Spanish at Medway and Maidstone College of Technology. He has written several text books on Spain and the Spanish language, and is co-compiler of the *Penguin Spanish Dictionary.*

T. A. R. HYNDMAN served as a barrister's clerk during the General Strike and helped to defend men charged for riotous disturbances. In 1936–7 he joined the International Brigade in Spain and in 1938 went on to Vienna, where he helped to thwart Gestapo activities. After the war, he worked in the theatre, first as a stage manager and then as a stage director. He took to drink, but was eventually rescued by the South Wales Council on Alcoholism. He now helps recovering alcoholics in Dyfrig House, Cardiff, works among addicts and depressives and is a regular visitor to offenders in Cardiff Prison.

J. H. BASSETT joined the Communist Party and went to Spain to fight in the Civil War. He spent most of the Second World War at the Royal Aircraft establishment at Farnborough, applying electronic techniques to the flight testing of aircraft and missiles. In 1949 he became the technical salesman for a large scientific instrument group, one of whose companies made microscopes. He became so interested in microscopy that he began to design his own microscopes and now runs his own distribution business.

Index